# THE
# NEGRO AND HIS NEEDS

# THE

# NEGRO AND HIS NEEDS

By

RAYMOND PATTERSON

WITH A FOREWORD

BY

WILLIAM HOWARD TAFT

*The Black Heritage Library Collection*

BOOKS FOR LIBRARIES PRESS

FREEPORT, NEW YORK

1971

First Published 1911
Reprinted 1971

Reprinted from a copy in the
Fisk University Library Negro Collection

INTERNATIONAL STANDARD BOOK NUMBER:
0-8369-8929-5


LIBRARY OF CONGRESS CATALOG CARD NUMBER:
74-178480


PRINTED IN THE UNITED STATES OF AMERICA
BY
NEW WORLD BOOK MANUFACTURING CO., INC.
HALLANDALE, FLORIDA 33009

# FOREWORD

Raymond Patterson was a classmate of mine at Yale. For years he was a leader among the newspaper correspondents at Washington. He was a man of great ability and showed it in his college life. He became a trained journalist. He was an earnest and close observer, and a conscientious historian. He was possessed of a judicial mind, and it manifested itself in his treatment of what he saw. He was a man of wide interests. The problems that the country has before it for solution commanded his close attention, not as a mere recorder of events, but as one who, by his suggestion and clear statement of the facts, could aid their solution.

The following pages are the result of his investigations into conditions surrounding the negro question at the South. They are full of interest for every one who believes that this question is the most serious, facing the American people. One need not concur in the conclusions which Mr. Patterson draws, to appreciate the value of the work he has done. He has been painstaking and conscientious. He has made his story most readable.

*Wm. H. Taft*

# PREFACE

The Southern man is too close to the negro and the Northern man too far away. Somewhere between these two widely different points of view must be found ultimately the solution of the negro problem. At the present time that problem is so complex, it has so many curious ramifications, it involves so many side issues, it concerns such vast interests for the welfare of mankind itself, that it should be approached with great deliberation. The adjustment of the relations between the black race and the white in America cannot be a matter of years, or even of generations, but of centuries. In the meantime, however, it is of vast importance to the country, as steps toward the ultimate solution, to solve some of the temporary problems regarding the coloured race—problems of education, of racial development, of political and economic status, above all, of methods of intellectual and moral culture by which the negro shall be helped to rise from his present low plane to a higher. With some of these problems it is the purpose of this book to deal.

REVISED BY
MRS. RAYMOND PATTERSON

# CONTENTS

## *THE COMPLEX PROBLEM*

## *A STUDY OF EXISTING CONDITIONS*

## *THE SOLUTION*

## *DEDUCTIONS*

# THE COMPLEX PROBLEM

# I

## The Problem of Increase

THE problem of numerical increase or diminution of the negro race in America is of vital importance in relation to the question of their ultimate destiny. Are the black people to go on increasing under the present aggravated conditions, thus rendering the situation more acute? Or, on the other hand, will they gradually be eliminated, either by the working of ordinary physical laws, or by the slow process of amalgamation?

Throughout the Southern States there has been a great disregard of the important work of keeping vital statistics, and people who are well informed on other subjects take it for granted that, because the negro is outclassing the whites in point of numbers in certain localities, his race is growing faster than that of his former masters. It is necessary to go to the cities for anything like accurate figures; and these do not sustain the view that the negroes are growing in numbers, substantially and generally, faster than the whites.

All the Southern States are peculiar, owing to the fact that there is practically no foreign immigration

in that section of the country.  There are a few of
the southern European immigrants, notably the
agricultural Italians, who could probably succeed in
the South and make money, but they do not like
to be placed in direct competition with the black
man, and thus far have not entered the South in any
large numbers.  The result is that the numerical
relations of the two races are largely dependent in
the South merely upon the natural ebb and flow of
humanity, caused by the inevitable processes of
birth and death.

It so happens that in the city of Charleston an
intelligent system of vital statistics has been
adopted, which has a direct bearing upon the race
question.  The figures show that while the negro
is reproducing himself much more rapidly than the
white, he is subjected to the usual great law of compensation, owing to the fact that his death rate is
also nearly double that of the white man.  For example, in one given year the mortality among the
whites was at the rate of one in fifty-two of the
population, as against one in twenty-seven among
the negroes.  And this is by no means the highest
proportion among the records of negro death rates
in that city.  Of course, if such a death rate as this
were the whole of the problem, the coloured race
would soon disappear, and the solution of the race
question would be merely a matter of patience on
the part of the whites.

The extraordinary mortality among the children of the negroes is something pitiful to contemplate. In the case of the figures just quoted, of the total of 1,153 negro deaths in the year referred to, no less than 391, or about one-third, were children under five years of age. Between five and ten the mortality is extremely small, the heaviest death rate, aside from that of the little children, falling between twenty and forty years. The negro children are born into the world with a large percentage of malformation; they are grossly neglected, suffer often from diseases of the eyes, and too often inherit from diseased parents maladies such as their forefathers never knew in the barbaric wilds of Africa.

A further study of the mortality statistics of Charleston, which is thoroughly representative of the coast cities of the South, develops the fact that the great negro death rate is from diseases directly traceable to improper food and unsanitary surroundings and associations. The negro, not only in the cities but everywhere else, is notoriously ignorant of the most ordinary laws of health, and seems to have reduced uncleanliness to a fine art. Trained students of vital statistics and all physicians will appreciate the fact that the negro is a tropical importation, and is in consequence immediately subjected to fatal affections of the throat and lungs. His natural predisposition is accentuated by the fact that he dresses himself improperly, takes but little care of his health, heeds no warnings, and is frequently content in the way of medical attention with efforts based on the grossest superstitions of his race. In the total of 1,153 deaths already quoted, the principal items of negro mortality show that tuberculosis was responsible for 177 deaths. Pneumonia claimed 95; Bright's disease, 128; apoplexy, 23; enteritis, 59; entero-colitis, 41; marasmus, 56; typhoid fever, 31; malarial fever, 25. It is therefore immediately evident that much of the enormous death rate among the negroes in the South is not climatic, but is the result of unhygienic personal habits and ignorance or utter disregard of the basic laws of health, combined with a racial predisposition. It naturally follows that if the negro could be taught to take care of himself (which many wise people believe to be impossible), the death rate among his race ought to drop down marvellously in the Southern States.

When one turns to the list of births, an equally startling and significant condition of affairs is at once discovered. The negro is reproducing himself, if the Charleston figures can be believed, at an extraordinary rate, which has thus far proved sufficient to offset the high mortality brought about by his ignorant defiance of the laws of hygiene. The negro population of Charleston is in the relation of about four to three to that of the whites. Instead of the birth rate being in the same proportion, however, it is found to be more than double that of the whites. The city of Charleston itself is not making any growth, but it will readily be seen that if the negro keeps up his present gait in the way of adding to the population, and at the same time becomes educated enough to avoid deaths caused by mere filth and lack of proper attention to health, the proportion between the blacks and the whites will be altered for the worse, and the aristocratic old cradle of the Confederacy will be turned over to the race of those who were originally its servants. And from other equally reliable figures is ascertained the striking fact that the negroes are increasing in the cities of the South, except in Washington, at a perceptibly faster rate than the whites.

Another point to be taken into consideration is the small but steady drift of the negroes both from country and city toward the North. The movement is not a large one, from the point of view of those who are accustomed to deal with the statistics of foreign immigration in this country, yet it has its own significance. For at every point in the South, most particularly in the purely agricultural sections, one hears the almost continual complaint, which at certain seasons of the year becomes strident, of the lack of labour. Hundreds and hundreds of thousands of acres of good land in the Southern States lie ready for the plough; but there is no man to hold it. And this lack of labour is not being re-

duced, as is the case in the North, by a constant
stream of foreign immigration.

There is, and every planter knows it, a little trick-
ling stream of darkies going day by day, more often
night by night, away from the warm, moist fields,
into the dark, dank, degraded hovels of the cities.
The negro drifts off in ones and twos and half-
dozens down the rivers and along the lines of the
railroads.  This movement is no more intelligent
than anything else the negro does.  It is not even
intuitive, because the agricultural negro in the South
is pretty well off, if he did but know it.  So the
country negro drifts to the city, and being uncouth
and unskilled to a degree not appreciated by Northern people, he finds his first employment in the most
menial and the hardest labour we have.

The children of this agricultural negro, however,
are city born and bred, and they learn to get places
a little bit better than their " dad " was satisfied
with.  Some of them become bricklayers, carpenters,
wheelwrights, and engage in similar skilled occupations, which bring to them good wages but no more
prosperity as a rule, because, with the negro, prosperity is not generally measured by the amount of
his wages.  From the city negro there gradually
grows up a little more cultivated class, among whom
one will find a large percentage of the mixed blood,
which seeks occupations directly on the railroads.

I have found from talks with humble but intelli-

gent coloured people that there is a general tendency
northward among this class, which is perhaps as yet
imperceptible to the white people. That is to say,
a Pullman porter who has run from New Orleans
to Mobile will after a limited time work his way
into a run from Mobile to Montgomery, and then
to Atlanta or Chattanooga, the end of his run being
evidently a little further north with every change
he makes. In this way, they tell me, the railroad
negroes are shifting North slowly but surely day
by day, and in the only way they could do it without directly buying a ticket and moving wife and
family.

When I asked the coloured people themselves for
an explanation as to this northward movement
among the railway class, it was at least noticeable
that all questions of politics were immediately eliminated. Most of them seem to have but vague ideas
on the ballot, and I firmly believe that the Southern
negro, however it may be with his Northern
brother, cares but little for the franchise, except as
he might care to have any bit of collateral. The
invariable answer to my inquiries as to why the
coloured people want to get North was the statement that the tips were larger and more frequent
than in the South.

These observations in the South are corroborated
by the figures in regard to the increase of the negro
population in the North, not only in the southern

Middle States, where the race riots and struggles most frequently occur, but in New England and the Northwest. Is there, then, a possibility that at some time more or less remote the race question will transfer itself, with all its complexities, from the cotton plantations of the South to the coal mines and wheat fields of the North?

## II

## The Problem of Temperament

PROBABLY no white man ever did or ever will fathom the depths and the shallows of the real negro's character and disposition. One frequently hears Southern people who have been " raised " by old-time mammies and who played in childhood with little black companions say with despairing frankness, " I've been watching the negro all these years, but I don't know him any better now than I did in the first place." Surely if the Southerners admit that the negro is a mystery to them, growing no more intelligible as the days go by, Northern people must be prepared for many race traits which cannot be accounted for by ordinary theorists.

The fact that seems generally forgotten by white people both North and South is that the negro is of a childhood race. The dark continent of Africa was evidently passed by in the march of civilization, and while the Caucasian and Mongolian races were striving painfully upward, the black race remained painfully near the starting-point. According to the judgment of those who have most conscien-

tiously studied the negro—planters, officers of the
law, philanthropists, school-teachers, negroes themselves—it is unfair even to consider the black man
in America except always in the light of the fact
that the most enlightened representatives of his race
are only a few generations away from actual barbarism, while the great mass of the blacks, embracing many millions of men, women, and children, is still far lower in the social and mental scale
than were the shepherds of Chaldea in the days of
Abraham.

Whenever a Southerner starts in to justify the
current local treatment of the negro, it is always by
dwelling upon the bad qualities of the black man.
And indeed even a casual observation must convince
a fair-minded person that almost any of the Southern negroes, left to themselves, will pilfer small
articles, will lie in the most inconsequential manner,
and will develop traits which seem to justify their
classification as downright savages.   The average
Southern negro is shiftless and improvident; he cannot save and he cannot anticipate.   He has but few
domestic ties, and in these few he shifts his allegiance with rare facility.   He is gifted in the matter
of intemperance, when he gets a chance, and as for
immorality, that of the original negro is so cath-
olic, so all pervasive that it cannot well be described.

If one looks lower, at the most debased class of
negroes, there are still blacker pictures to be painted,

whose colours can be laid on with sombre horror and with entire fidelity to truth. Here responsibility for human life is not even understood, and they kill each other for trivial causes. When arraigned for the crime of murder they will admit the killing, but will assign reasons for it so extravagantly childish as to make one doubt whether the reasons are not cunningly invented to hide with a veil of innocence a deeper tragedy. In one little country town the district attorney has on the average one case a week, during the season when the court is in session, of a negro murdering another negro. It is not hard to find the blackest and most savage of crimes, infanticide, incest of most complicated character, and other offences committed only by savages.

This dismal calendar of crime shows an extreme point of view in regard to the immorality and criminality of the negro; true, because painted by those who ought to know him best, and who in fact make more allowances for his failures than do those who know him least. Yet when one begins to analyze this extreme condition, it is at once easy to see, aside from mere race prejudice, that the negro is no better and no worse than any other savage. His sins of immorality, shocking to so many, are the sins of the untutored animal. He has as many domestic ties as the noblest horse or the most faithful dog. He will pilfer, just as a highly bred dog will occasionally steal a piece of meat from a butcher's block; he will tell foolish lies as a little child does, partially through fright, partially through a low species of barbaric cunning, but oftenest through downright ignorance.

You can go anywhere into the South where the negro is most himself and find the Southern people themselves lauding to the skies the absolute fidelity of the " ole-time " negro. Now, the " ole-time " negro was nothing more or less than the African savage or the son of a savage, forced to work at the command of a white man who had been for five thousand years his superior. To-day, everywhere in the South, there are trusts reposed in poor ignorant negroes who can neither read nor write, and those trusts are seldom if ever betrayed. Go where you will, and you can find the white planter putting up a sack of corn to pay his negroes in the field, and sending it out alone and unprotected in the custody of a black man astride of a mule. In all the lynchings, none is ever provoked by a breach of trust on the part of the humble negro.

The negroes are not treacherous; they do not, in emulation of the Indian or of the Irish peasant, take pot-shots at harsh and hated landlords from behind wayside hedges. After a century of horrible slavery, the black man in America never made the slightest attempt to destroy his former master. The negro is a good worker. His mind works slowly, as a matter of course, but he imitates rapidly and successfully. Unfortunately, he has imitated some of the vices of the white man, and some of the counts in the indictment against the negro should really be charged to the superior race, from whom he borrowed them.

There are strange limitations to the original negro mind, but in the ultimate analysis these limitations will be found inherent in any race which is in the childhood condition as regards the world at large. The negro appears to bear but slight resentment to ill treatment, but on the other hand it is difficult to arouse in him a continuing sense of real gratitude. Both of these failures in his mental grasp can readily be traced to his lack of a trained memory. He forgets in the morning the favour done him the night before, but he is equally forgetful of the injury done at the same time.

A faithful study of these characteristics should convince any one that they are essentially similar to the mental grasp of a little child who has not learned the world, who cannot readily distinguish friend from foe, who frequently conceives himself to be injured when things are being done for his own good, and who will forget his delight of the morning in his distaste of the afternoon. Yet in spite of this obvious likeness, it is an impressive fact that all through the hospitable Southland are men and women of culture who declare in all good

faith, backing up their declaration with some spe-
cious argument, that the negro is hopeless, that
education of any kind spoils him, and that he is a
satisfactory part of the mechanism of the world
only when he is most nearly a downright barbarian.

Now if the negro cannot be bettered by a reasonable process of education, if his unmorality and
his animalism cannot be dissipated by patient care
and wise instruction, our own civilization is a failure.  The negro must be developed mentally and
morally and his development must come by contact
with the whites, a contact which in the present state
of things hardly exists.  For example, I know one
plantation where one man, the white superintendent,
occupied the great house in solitary magnificence,
with five hundred and fifty negroes under him.  So
far as I could learn, there was not a school on that
plantation; if there was, I did not see it and no
one mentioned it.  The sole impulse toward civilization for half a thousand negroes lay in the uncon-
scious and oftentimes unguarded influence of a
solitary white man, who was by no means of a high
grade, from an educational standpoint, though socially a courteous, affable gentleman.

The negro, as I have come to believe, is not at
present capable of any high degree of education,
except in a few isolated cases.  But it is preposter-
ous and out of harmony with the broad scheme of
American government to assert that the negro must

be left just where he was when he came from
Africa, or that he becomes contaminated and degenerated by contact with the whites.  Nothing
could be farther from the truth.  Every little schoolhouse, in the South as in the North, is doing its
silent and unnoticed work.  The uplifting of the
negro is not the work of yesterday or to-day or to-
morrow, but of the long years and the fruitful centuries to come.

There is a vein of tropical imagination in the
negro which has never yet been worked to its legitimate limit.  He responds ultimately to patient endeavour, provided one can arrest his enthusiasm in
the right way.  The religion of the black man—in
this I refer to the ignorant negro of the fields and
not the cultivated negro of the schools—the black
man's religion is exuberant and florid.  It is still
tinged with the most curious superstitions, but back
of all this is a sentimentality which might readily
make a devotee under proper direction.  Grafted
upon the sacred truths of Christianity are quaint
bits of voodooism, and the Methodist Protestant
minister still runs in sharp competition to the snake
doctor, the herb woman, and the moonlight maker
of black magic.

I know of one case where a young man in abject
terror complained to the local authorities because
his uncle had gone away to town for the express
purpose of buying a witch candle, which, when

lighted, would measure the span of life of the trembling complainant.  He fully believed that unless the white man's law could be brought to bear, his breath would be cut off with the last expiring gasp of the witch candle his uncle would bring from town.

Such superstitions, and much more curious ones, are openly referred to in many a plantation pulpit, and I know of several cases where the shepherd of a flock has declared that acts of immorality between members of the same church are entirely without sin, whereas, if committed between a church member and an outsider, they would end in the eternal damnation of both.  There are dusky pastors who run riot through a plantation because of a curious twisting of a certain biblical text concerning their prerogatives among the female members of the flock.  Yet all these appear to be but mere barbaric gropings after a still better and more emotional religion.

Dr. Booker T. Washington, asked for his personal opinion as to the particular tendency or capacity of the negro, as a guide for his future treatment, replied without hesitation, in words which throw an interesting sidelight upon this question of the negro temperament:

" The negro's most prominent trait undoubtedly is his imagination.  This might cause a tendency in the race later on toward music, poetry, and the arts. Just now, however, the imaginative faculty seems to lead the negro chiefly toward oratory. His imagination finds its readiest outlet in fluency of talk and this probably accounts for the popularity of politics with some negroes, while in others this racial trait finds expression in the number of those who take up preaching as a congenial profession, in which they can exercise their gift of oratory and appeal to the imagination and emotions of their audiences."

# III

## The Mulatto

ONE question of interest in the study of the possibilities of the negro is that of the relative mental and physical qualifications of the mulatto as compared with the pure-blooded negro. Professor DuBois, of the University of Atlanta, himself one of the mixed race and one of the finest specimens of a cultivated negro, has made a thoughtful analysis of the situation.

" There is no essential mental difference," he says, " between the mixed breed and the negro, and the two different charges made against the mulatto are sufficient evidence of this fact. In the first place, the Southern white people constantly assert that all that has been accomplished by the negro has been done by men of mixed blood, and that after all it is only the white strain showing. In the same breath our critics assert that the mulatto is responsible for the vices of the negro, and that he is a mental and moral degenerate. The two assertions are frequently heard from the same men at the same time, and they only go to show what I have asserted, that the mulatto is no better and no worse than the pure

negro. By mulatto I mean, of course, the mixed
breed, because the variations as to the colour strain
on the one side or the other are becoming too complicated to permit us to follow the white strain
down to the last drop.

" The mulattoes or mixed race have had an advantage of the black negro amounting to about a
generation, merely as a matter of environment. The
yellow boys and girls in slavery days were not so
regularly put to work in the fields, but were generally selected for house servants, and were frequently brought to the cities and put to work in
house service and in hotels as messengers and in
similar employments. It thus generally happened
that the mixed race was thrown more in contact
with the educated whites, and so gradually learned
a little of education, a little imitation refinement,
and some beginnings of culture. They were imitative, and learned a good deal from this association with white people, so that, taken as a whole,
the mixed race found itself in advance of the pure
negro.

" This advantage of the mulatto was a matter of
association merely. In men as in animals it may
be presumed that breeding will tell, and to a slight
extent therefore the white blood tends to make the
mulatto slightly more acute than his negro blood,
but in point of fact it is practically difficult to trace
the difference."

Professor DuBois went on to show the photograph of a class recently graduated from Atlanta University, quite the average and typical of the usual class. He pointed out the honour students among them. " Here," he said, " is a girl so nearly white you could scarcely tell the difference; another with white features and a dusky skin. Here also is a pure black, thick-lipped negro boy, and another, black, but with nearly Caucasian features. This picture shows that out of an average class the students who are distinguished above their fellows represent every grade, from the undeniable negro type to the girl who could pass muster as white in almost any Northern city.

" Mixture of the races is not to be feared in itself," Professor DuBois continued. " What is to be feared is the mixture of the bad elements in both races. If you take a vicious white man and a vicious negro and mix them together, the offspring will naturally be vicious, not because he is a mulatto, but because his parentage is bad. The safety of the whites, as far as the process of amalgamation is concerned, lies in the uplifting of the negro race. As the negroes become more educated, as they acquire a pride in their own society, illicit association with the white man ceases more and more, and this is the principal reason why the process of amalgamation, which was quite rapid a generation ago, has now become considerably reduced.

" Many of the shortcomings charged to the mulatto might easily be ascribed to the notorious degeneracy of illegitimate children.  As the tone of the coloured race is raised, the connection between white and black will necessarily be more and more among the most vicious of the coloured people, and hence it is to the interest of everybody to upbuild the coloured race as rapidly as possible, to strengthen their moral tone, and thus to remove them from surroundings where they become victims of the vicious elements among the whites.

" Here in the South to-day there is comparatively little mixture of the races in the larger cities, but the process is going on to some extent in the smaller towns, and in many an instance a prudent negro mother finds it wise to send her good-looking yellow daughter to some institution to save her from the temptation of association with the lowest grade of white boys in the neighbourhood."

The other side of the question, that of attributing all the achievements of the negro to his " white strain," I heard discussed by Booker Washington, himself an exponent of the accepted mulatto type. He never knew his father and is ignorant of his identity, having been born in slavery; but he is quite light-coloured, and would readily pass for an educated Cuban or South American.  He is keenly alive to the importance of the question as frequently discussed in magazines and newspapers regarding the supposed mental, moral, and physical degeneracy of the mixed race.

" I cannot see," he said, " that there is any great difference between the mental capacity of the pure-blooded negro and that of a man of a mixed race.

" Among the distinct negro types that are black rather than of mixed blood, who have done most brilliant work in real life, are educators like William J. Edwards, principal of the Normal and Industrial Institute at Snow Hill, Alabama; Isaac Fisher, principal of the Branch Normal College at Pine Bluff, Arkansas; Lizzie E. Wright, principal of the Voorhees Normal and Industrial Institute at Denmark, South Carolina; C. L. Marshall, principal of the Christiansburg Normal and Industrial Institute at Cambria, Virginia; and William H. Holtzclaw, principal of the Utica Normal and Industrial Institute at Utica, Mississippi. Right here in Tuskegee we have another evidence in the person of George W. Carver, the head of the agricultural department, who is an accurate scientist, trained under the personal supervision of James Wilson, Secretary of Agriculture, who was formerly at the head of the Iowa State Agricultural College at Ames, Iowa.

" All these and many other men of pure negro blood have apparently demonstrated that whatever achievements are made by the negroes are not to be

credited to any white blood they have, but to their
perseverance in securing a good education.

" As to the physical difference between the mulatto and the pure-bred negro, there is considerable
diversity of opinion, but there are no reliable figures
to prove that a man of mixed blood is either weaker
or stronger than his black brother."

Some years ago much attention was attracted by
an article, which attempted to show that the mulattoes were chiefly responsible for the unrest then
existing among the negroes.  The author was Mr.
Alfred H. Stone, a cotton planter of Greenville,
Mississippi, a Southerner of wide personal experience among the negroes, a careful student of the
race problem, and singularly free from prejudice.
He told me that he was becoming more and more
convinced that it is the mulatto who must be dealt
with by the white man rather than the pure negro,
who is, he asserts, blindly following the lead of his
hybrid brother.

" The mulatto is not a degenerate," he said; " on
the contrary, the mixed blood is far superior to the
negro.  The mulatto may solve the race question
for us some day.  The time is coming, and it is not
so far off, when there will be a breaking up of old
associations and the mulatto and the negro will for-
ever separate.  This is the condition now in many
of the West India Islands, and my observation is
that we are drifting into the same condition of

affairs. The mulatto is all powerful in the negro community to-day. His influence is dominant either for good or for evil.

"I am quite aware of the fact that well-known mulatto leaders like Booker T. Washington and Professor DuBois constantly declare in public that there is no difference between the pure negro and the man of mixed blood. I believe, however, that they make these statements more as a matter of policy and to unite the race, although in their heart of hearts they know and believe that the white strain does tell and that practically all the men of so-called negro blood who have done anything in the world are of the mulatto type.

"From my personal talk with the men of the mixed blood, I am convinced that they all feel the degradation involved in being put into the same class with the black field hand. I know that many mulattoes feel sore about this, and while they continue to assert the oneness of the negro race, for obvious reasons of policy, in private conversation they inevitably lay stress upon their blood relation to the white man, and constantly call attention to their white ancestry.

"So far as concerns the truth of my contention that it is the mulatto who is the cause of dissension and unrest among the negroes, I am willing to leave that to the judgment of any fair man who will take the trouble to go over the files of representative

negro journals and magazines. He will find that
these papers are published by mulattoes, and are a
source of great danger and positive menace to anything like permanent good relations between the
races, making as they do constant appeals to passion and hate, and parading and exaggerating griev-
ances and wrongs. The editor of one paper, probably the worst, is called a negro, but is really a combination of Indian, negro, and white man. As a
factor for creating strife and ill-feeling, I will
match him as a mulatto against any two dozen pure
negroes Mr. Washington can produce in America."

Mr. Stone corroborated what I was told all over
the South, that the amalgamation of the black and
the white races is rapidly disappearing.

" There was a vast amount of this amalgamation,"
he said, " up to perhaps twenty years ago. Since
then there has been a decided change of sentiment
on the part of Southern white men. I know that
not so long ago it was not an uncommon thing to
find an overseer or superintendent on a plantation
who would have from one to half a dozen con-
cubines. This practice has practically been done
away with. The planters will not permit their overseers to do such things, and the overseers themselves seldom offend in this regard, although they
are placed in an extraordinary position, frequently
being the only white persons in a great multitude
of coloured people. The mixture of the races is

quite evidently dying out, at least for the present, and this increases the importance of the mulatto, and renders it easier for him to assume actual leadership."

Whether the mulatto's ability is vastly superior to that of the black negro, will be an open question for many years to come. But there is a curious vein of vanity that enters into his influence in the negro community, which is unquestioned, and which is, after all, universally human. I refer to his acknowledged good looks, which invariably command the childish and boastful admiration of the blacks, and which make for popularity, and, naturally, add to his influence.

The coloured woman, who by various and mysterious methods, straightens the kinks out of her wool for the time being, may be loudly denounced by her less successful sisters, but they invariably believe her achievement to be one more step toward the beauty of the whites!

The traditional " ole time darkey," whose passing the Southerner constantly mourns, is the black man or woman, nine cases out of ten, rather than the light-coloured or " brown-skinned " servant. The mulatto may have the ambition, with its common discontent and restlessness, due to his white strain, but he has no more energy, if as much, and, generally speaking, far less conscientious thoroughness, than his pure black brother.

## IV

## The Problem of Immorality

ONE of the things which would strike the most casual observer is the persistence with which the white men who are undeniably good friends of the negroes represent the entire black race as being grossly immoral and difficult to deal with. At all times and in all places, from the most intelligent, the most impartial, and the most shrewd white observers in the South, one hears that a negro man, as well as a negro woman, is absolutely devoid of the slightest idea of morality, that he is constantly degenerating, and that he is becoming more and more a brute every day.

There must be something in these statements, because, otherwise, they would not be repeated so persistently, and by men whose opinion is entitled to all respect. Nevertheless, a casual and possibly superficial examination of the life and condition of the negroes in the cities does not seem to bear out the statements at all. I have been into negro slums in most of the large cities of the South, and I have arrived at the conclusion, based on what I have seen, that the so-called criminal classes among the negroes

are as an average far more law-abiding, far less
noisy, far more apt to have their fun by themselves
than the similar class in white slums in Northern
cities. This observation will probably be resented
by Southern men, but it is honestly made, after
studying the most debased class of negroes, who
are admittedly in the cities. However debased they
may be in their private life, the side they show to
the casual observer leads me to believe that they
are not nearly so black as they are painted.

In New Orleans, for example, beside studying
the roustabout negro on the great levee which was
once the glory of the Crescent City, I spent an evening investigating some of the worst of the negro
sections. I came out of the little expedition greatly
surprised at the comparative decency and good order of the alleged debased negroes. There was once
an alderman in New Orleans by the name of Story,
who conceived the idea of confining the disreputable
class, both white and coloured, to a certain section
of the city. His idea was successfully carried out;
but unfortunately for him, the people persisted in
calling that section of New Orleans "Storyville,"
and so it is known to this day. On my way to the
distinctly negro section I was brought face to face
with the most flagrant exhibition of the social evil
among the whites I have ever seen in any city of
the United States.

For several city blocks there is a continuous line

of little houses, each of which is occupied by a white woman, who stands at the door all the evening long in short skirts, with bare arms and extravagantly décolleté dresses, if such one can call the garments these women affect. Such a startling exhibition of vice and debauchery as this, such open solicitation from the doorsteps, such an outrageous exhibition in public by gaslight of unadorned female charms, would not be permitted in New York or Chicago for fifteen minutes. The worst episodes in the Tenderloin are a Sunday-school compared to a five-minute walk through the most populous section of Storyville in New Orleans.

Having passed through this experience, I was most agreeably surprised to find that my destination, a negro gambling house, dance hall, saloon, and crap-shooting parlour, all under one roof, was an exceedingly tame affair. In that joint, among the most debased class of negroes in the city, I spent a considerable time, and there was not a suspicion of a fight, nor anything which even approached the extravagant white debauchery a block further up the street. Men and women came in and out, a little gambling was going on in an interior room, there was some drinking at the bar, a good deal of familiarity between the two sexes, and an occasional exposé of gaudy hosiery with *malice intente,* but for the most part, the exhibition was simply downright stupid vulgarity. I do not doubt that this negro establishment could be excelled for indecency by any similar establishment among the whites in almost any city of fifty thousand or more inhabitants.

It was here that I met Felix. That was the only name he responded to. He was one of the managers of the place, a shrewd, intelligent negro, who talked a curious *patois,* derived in equal quantities from his French father and his negro mother. Leaning up against the penny-in-the-slot gambling machine, he gave me the only practical suggestion I have yet heard regarding the question of lynching for criminal assault. Without the idioms of the dialect, what he said was somewhat as follows:

" I have not always been able to understand this assault business, and I do not quite understand it yet. I think every man who assaults a woman ought to have his life taken away from him, and the sooner the better. Just what makes our people make assaults I cannot tell you. As to that, it seems to be in the blood of some black people. I think you will find that the men who commit this terrible act are almost always very black men, very big men, and very ignorant men; in almost every case they are negroes brought up in the fields and who know but little about civilized life. You will seldom hear of a mulatto assaulting either a white woman or a black woman. I believe the men who commit this crime ought to be hanged right away, but they ought not to be lynched. The only excuse for lynching I have ever heard is that the law is so slow in its operation. That is true, but it could easily be fixed. It would be a simple matter to pass a law giving the coroner's jury authority, in cases of assault, to determine the guilt of the person, and if he were found guilty, to execute him within twenty-four hours. That would have a much better effect upon the black people who are addicted to those crimes than lynching ever could have. Many black people are so stirred up at the injustice of a lynching party that they forget the fact that the man deserves to die for the beastly crime he committed. If some quick action according to law, like the one I have suggested, could be adopted, the terror to the negro would be just the same, and the white men would not have constantly to defend themselves for defying the law which they themselves make, and which they will not permit us either to make or to change."

There seems a great deal of reason in these suggestions, especially as they came from a man who was at that minute overlooking a crowd of debased negro hoodlums of the class which might commit such crimes. I encouraged him to give me some more of his short-range criminal experience, and in reply he said what every person in the South knows to be true:

" In most cases the right man is lynched, I guess, but we coloured people know that in many other

cases they get the wrong man and he is hanged just
the same, or burned just the same, or shot just the
same as if he had done something. That is what
makes the coloured people so resentful, even in case
of the lynching of one of their number who has
really committed an assault. I know of a case myself out in the country here, where there was a poor
black man in the cornfield at work. He did not
know there was anybody near him, but in working
through the corn he made more or less noise, as a
matter of course. A young white girl who was passing by took fright, and running to the nearest house
reported that a negro had jumped at her. A crowd
was gathered together; they had their guns, and the
first thing that poor negro knew he was captured.
He had not even seen the girl, and did not understand why he had been pursued. Nevertheless, he
was hanged just the same. That was a mistake on
the part of a mob, to be sure, but it was a mistake
that happens too often, and every such mistake
makes the coloured people who know of it more
angry, more resentful, more disposed to commit
such crimes than they were before."

Felix had a theory all his own that the black
negro is inferior to the mulatto in intelligence, in
capacity for education, and in morals. He believed
that the black people know this, and seek the society
of the mulatto as the next thing to that of the
white man. "The white strain tells every time,"

he insisted. But then, Felix was half French, and probably prejudiced.

It was from this same Felix that I learned also of the widespread and constantly increasing use of cocaine in various forms among the more debased negroes, and of the growing indulgence in all kinds of alcoholic stimulants among negro women. It is interesting, too, to know that the negro in the South has long since stopped carrying a razor, and now carries a pistol. My friend pointed out a half-dozen roughly clad, big, burly negro roustabouts, every one of whom, he declared, had a pistol inside his shirt, some of them two. This, like some other bad characteristics of the negro, may be traced to the deficient civilization of the South itself. That is, the pistol-carrying custom is a direct imitation of the white man's habit, and is in itself responsible for many brutal killings.

It is in this same spirit of imitation that the negro so frequently assumes an offensive strut or swagger, intended really to be a copy of the independent walk of the white man whom he acknowledges to be so vastly his superior as to stir him to emulation. That white man has not taught him morality, either; if he has, how can one account for the numberless thousands of men and women of mixed race, some old enough to date back to the " good old slavery days " and others the manifest product of a deficient moral sentiment on the part of the white man to-

day? Few mulattoes walk the earth whose strain
of white blood was introduced into their veins
through the medium of lawful wedlock, and if the
negro of the fields is immoral to an atrocious degree, and I am not disposed to deny it, every mulatto he meets is a reminder to him of the fact
that certain white men, in spite of their boasted
civilization, have no higher standard of morality
than this ignorant black savage who hoes the cotton
and the corn all day long, who laughs half the
night through, and who knows little of care and
less of morality.

What may be made even of the debased class of
negroes, under proper enforcement of law, is evi-
denced in the curious old city of Charleston, the
" cradle of the Confederacy," with its gentle flavour
of mild decay. It is not a lively place in summer,
but it is at that season that the coloured people
flock into the town. I was sitting one hot day in
the mayor's office when the chief of police came in
with a report that there were in his opinion 2,500
more idle negroes in the city than there were a year
before, thus calling for unusual police vigilance. In
number the negroes of Charleston far exceed the
whites, and they are notably quiet. Walking late
at night through the negro quarter, I found far less
disturbance than one would find in a corresponding
quarter among the bitterly poor in New York or
Chicago.

Within sight of Fort Sumter negro policemen patrol their beats and perform their duties to the entire satisfaction of the authorities. One even rose to the distinction of becoming a lieutenant, in command of white men yet without ill feeling. On the whole, whatever may be thought or said as to the morality or immorality of the negroes, it cannot be asserted that they are distinctly vicious or dangerous to the public peace as a whole. On the contrary, they are naturally docile and peaceable. This may or may not be due to the fact that they know that punishment, swift and sure, will follow any serious offence, without much regard to the law's delays, and indeed without much regard to the law itself.

As to the general moral condition of the negro race in the South, I was one day fortunate enough to hear a discussion by Governor Sanders of Louisiana, originator of the " grandfather clause " and a native of the Bayou State. The state of things as he saw it was deplorable. " Nothing has ever been known," he said, " like the rapid degeneracy of the negro in the last twenty or thirty years. It is almost unbelievable, and cannot yet be comprehended by any one who has not watched it day by day. The negroes are rapidly drifting toward the cities, leaving the country never to return. The degenerate class of negroes is becoming addicted to all possible vices and drug habits, using whiskey, cocaine, mor-

phine, and similar things.  Out of a thousand negroes you would find at least seven hundred afflicted
with the vilest contagious diseases, which are being
transmitted to countless children.

"These negroes are infinitely worse than the
worst of their race twenty years ago.  During the
war-times the white people left their mothers, their
wives, their sweethearts, their children to the care
of the old-time negroes.  They never betrayed their
trust, and there was never a case of violence to
women or actual loss to property, although every
able-bodied white man was away in the army."

Following up this thought, Mr. Sanders with considerable impressiveness voiced the common fear
one hears about the South, which is always expressed as a justification for stern measures.

"What we are going to do when the last safe-
guard of these old-time negro people is gone I don't
know.  Their loyalty is beyond question, and with
that class of negro there is no trouble.  Why, some
of the old negroes still travel fifty miles to see my
old father, and he has them up on the gallery of the
house, where they talk for hours of the old days in
the parish, recalling incidents of forty, fifty, and
even sixty years ago.  But the white man in the
South to-day is constantly pursued by the awful
nightmare of the danger to women and children in
those sections where fiendish crimes are reported,
and no one knows just how fast or how far this

mania among the black people for assaults upon the life and honour of white women will go. Lynching does not seem to frighten these brutes, and the outlook for the future appears to have nothing in it except through the extermination or the deportation of the negro."

I suggested that if the negroes were diffused throughout the country so that they would form only a small percentage of the population in any one place, thus breaking down the dangerous congestion of the blacks in the South, it would possibly solve the problem. I was surprised, however, when the clear-headed sugar planter, lawyer, and legislator advanced an entirely new idea in this direction, which may or may not be sound in principle, but which is none the less the point of view of an acute, even if he may be a prejudiced, observer.

"Diffusion of the negro will never help matters, and I will tell you why. You will find that conditions in the hill country of Louisiana, Alabama, Georgia, and the Carolinas are practically the same. In none of these sections does the negro dominate in point of numbers. The black man is concentrated along the alluvial bottomlands, and in those sections he largely outnumbers the whites. In the hill country, where the whites outnumber the blacks, far different conditions prevail from those prevalent in the bottomlands.

"In the cotton country upon the hills, Tom

Brown, the white man, and Tom Jones, the black man, have farms side by side. They do the same work in the field, borrow and lend ploughs and other implements, and their women swap corn meal over the fence. Theoretically, there is neither social nor political equality, but the white and the black are thrown together in a way which has a disastrous effect upon the young buck negro whose father is perhaps one of the better class. The young black man Jones sees the white Miss Brown doing about the same work as his sister, and living on terms of actual industrial equality. He makes advances much as a white boy might, and is repulsed in disgust and reminded of the social differences he has forgotten. Then his savage blood flames up, and he takes by force what he can't have by consent and gratifies his lust at the expense of the poor, honest, virtuous white girl. Then the white men gather quickly, and hang the negro or perhaps burn him, as they have done in Delaware and in Illinois. That is what association on terms of apparent equality invariably does for the negro.

" In my home at St. Mary's Parish, and in all other sections where the black man largely outnumbers the white, the conditions are almost exactly the reverse. In the real black belt you seldom hear of these horrible cases which in other sections seem to be on the increase. With us the negroes never see the white people on anything like terms of equality.  The planter, the overseer, and all the white people about the place ride on horses, while the negro walks.  The black man seldom sees the women of the plantations, except in their carriages. The effect of all this is that the negro recognizes the white man as a superior being, and it never occurs to him to offer any indignity, much less to attempt violence against the superior race.

"Is it any wonder that the old-time lust of blood sometimes strikes in on the white people, as they see the old-fashioned negro disappearing, and crimes of inconceivable brutality increasing, while the negro is degenerating into a debased animal?"

# V

## The Problem of Environment

LET any Northern man stand on the levee of
the little plantation town of St. Joseph,
Louisiana, and watch the antics of two or
three thousand negroes, more or less inebriated, and
he will be likely to change his mind as to the simplicity of the negro question in the South. And if
he will linger there till after nightfall, he will begin
to understand the serious social equation the Southern people have been called to solve, and the difficulty of applying ordinary mathematics to it.

This picturesque little town of St. Joseph is an
aggregation of the houses of more or less wealthy
planters, with a vast population around them of
black labourers, all engaged in cultivating the great
staple, cotton, with a few patches here and there of
such corn as may be necessary to supply meal. To
reach the place one must go either to Vicksburg or
Natchez by rail, and from there journey on a Mississippi packet which lands one on the banks of the
great river after dark. It is so hard to get from
St. Joseph to any other place that the negroes here
have been left nearly as they were fifty years ago.

They are perfectly free; they can pick up and leave the town whenever they see fit, since there are no contracts, no laws, no public sentiment to hold them in the vicinity. But they are merely so far away from the railroad that they have remained here, and are an interesting social study, because typical of the original, unadulterated negro of slavery times, untouched by close association with white people.

I was fortunate enough to happen into the town on the Fourth of July, and to see a spontaneous but perfectly peaceable negro celebration. There were no firecrackers, there was no noise, except the loud laughter of the happiest, most light-hearted race the sun shines on. In the sunny South fireworks are reserved for Christmas time, when the negro is paid off. The Fourth of July is not widely celebrated by the whites, but the negroes claim it as a holiday. The ordinary custom gives a half holiday on every Saturday and a whole holiday on Sunday, so that it is a happy year for the planters when the Fourth comes on a Saturday, thus allowing the whole of Sunday for the sobering-up process.

The principal attraction of the negro Fourth of July was the ball game in the afternoon between two rival nines, which played on a white man's field just at the edge of town, and the spectators of which filled the white man's grandstand. It is the custom also to have a white man for umpire on these occasions, because otherwise that official is in danger of losing his life before the end of the game.

Both nines appeared on the field in their stocking feet, with the exception of one or two star players on each side, who preferred the bare skin underneath. The stockings were utilized as a kind of uniform, and the darkey who could produce the loudest and most violently striped hose was the particular pet of the grandstand. A few had on knickerbockers, but most of them rolled their ordinary trousers to the knees and then tucked them into their gaudy stockings. The effect of this was frequently ludicrous, because the negroes in this section of Louisiana are addicted to an article of clothing known as the "Wagner Pants." These are a species of trousers which are extremely wide over the foot, after the style affected by sailors. When the lower extremities of a pair of these "Wagner Pants" (for which, by the way, the darkies will pay more than for any other variety) are stuffed into a pair of red, yellow, and green socks, the effect is startling.

The baseball of the plantation negro is not half so bad as one might expect, and, except for the grotesque shouting of the participants, varied with lively dialogues between the first baseman and the spectators, it might easily have been an afternoon game between country teams in the North.

It was merely the prelude, however, of the real

business of the day, and simply served to sharpen the appetite for the determined attack made upon the whiskey barrels in the village stores. It is the habit of the darkies every Saturday to come into town in the afternoon and spend all the money they can beg, borrow, or steal for whiskey, and in this respect the negro women have become the greatest offenders.

All the afternoon a perfect stream of Afro-American women flowed into the town, and it was surprising to note how well dressed they were. The colours were of the most extraordinary combinations, the millinery could only have been concocted in a dream, but the general effect was remarkably good. On the whole, the plantation darkies when they first arrive in town will impress one more favourably than the same number of foreigners from the 'way-back agricultural counties upon a similar holiday. The negro women made a brave showing in the grandstand at the ball game, for a few innings, but they rapidly drifted down town, and before the afternoon was well spent the better part of them was far on the way toward a condition of gross intoxication.

The scenes in the little town after dark were not at all pleasant. As I stood on the " gallery " of Moore's big supply store I saw full fifty young women in a state of beastly intoxication, smoking pipes, cigars, and cigarettes, or chewing plug tobacco, staggering about the streets, being helped into the buggies in which they came, or openly making love in the most disgusting manner to their black-skinned sweethearts. Some of them, both men and women, were completely overcome, and had been rolled into corners to sleep it off, while one black man, quite gorgeously arrayed, was sleeping the sleep of the just, rolled across a barrel, his head and feet both on the floor.

The remarkable thing about this wholesale debauch was the fact that there were no serious fights. There were only a few white people in the town, but no negro offered the slightest indignity to any white man. They quarrelled among themselves constantly, to be sure, but these were only ordinary drunken wrangles, almost invariably between a man and the woman whom for the time being he called his wife. She never, it seemed, wanted to go home when he did, and if they came in a buggy, as many did, the pair were obliged to submit to arbitration before they could decide when to unhitch the mule and start homeward. The general peaceableness of the day was all the more surprising in view of the fact that a large proportion of these negroes carried pistols. Among white men of the same debased class, the combination of whiskey and pistols would have been sure to result disastrously.

After they left the town, a large percentage of the celebrants went on to a nearby cross-road where

there was a big dance and other festivities. At
this last place the crowd used up all the whiskey,
and then proceeded to purchase at famine prices the
entire stock of brandied cherries the store could produce. The whole debauch was shocking, and I have
detailed it merely to show the kind of negro with
whom the Southern planter has to deal. For this
Fourth of July episode is by no means extraordinary. It is repeated every Saturday night in a
minor degree, and on some special occasions becomes much more serious.

The plantation negro will go a long way for a
bottle of whiskey. Especially among the women
the drink craze has taken such possession that they
seem to have but two ambitions in life, to adorn
themselves in bright-coloured calico, and to drink
themselves into quarrelsome inactivity. On the
plantations it is the women who are most certainly
degenerating. They will not work in the fields any
more, so that the earning capacity of the family
is decidedly reduced. They have even stopped taking care of the little garden patch which is the salvation of the household when the salt pork runs low,
and to all intents and purposes seem determined to
become mere dusky butterflies of existence.

This degeneracy among the women is giving a
great deal of concern to those white people who
have the best interests of the negro at heart, and
the lack of character among the women of the

plantation class is not a thing which can readily be
described.  Few of them are married more legally
than they were during the slavery days.  In some
cases they are induced to go through the ceremony
by the promise of a more or less public wedding,
but even then the matrimonial tie is never the tie
that binds on a plantation.  Both men and women
drift apart without much ceremony, and one can
frequently find a family of half a dozen little children of various degrees of blackness, all owning
a common mother, but each permitted to claim an
entirely different paternal ancestor.  The cabins on
the plantation are built for two grown people and
an indefinite number of children, but the heads of
the household shift about in a remarkable fashion,
and even when a husband and wife live together
nominally, serious scandals are generally set afloat
in the community regarding both parties to the contract.

The white people find it impossible to regulate this
matter at all.  One pious woman insisted that she
would not have any grown negroes on her plantation who could not produce a marriage license.  She
was quite firm until the superintendent told her that
it would cost her about two hundred tenants, and
as it would be so difficult, if not impossible, to supply their places, the overseer would feel obliged to
resign.

Yet with all their debauchery, with all their lack

of real domestic ties, with all their pilfering, their lying, and their manifold shiftlessness, the plantation darkies in Louisiana are the happiest, most contented people in the world.  They make no complaints of their treatment, and their desires and ambitions are few.  When I asked one of the most intelligent foremen on one of the plantations what was the nicest thing to have, he promptly declared that it would be six bottles of whiskey.

The ground in this vicinity is so extravagantly rich that some sort of a crop can be produced with the slightest effort.  The country is entirely cut up with bayous and lakes, which are filled with fish. Fuel is free to the negro, he can keep his own cow and chickens, he has his own garden patch, and if he works at all it is only because the white man pushes him into it.

The negro " cabin " is not really a cabin at all, as most people think of it, but a one-story cottage.  It is not built of logs, nor is it a hut; it is a house built upon piles, weather-boarded, shingled, with a roof sloping both ways, front and back.  It generally has a porch, or " gallery " as the South calls it, across the entire front.  Inside there is only one room, with a pretty good-looking wooden bed, a bureau with a looking-glass, but not much other furniture.  These articles, which constitute the bedroom part of the house, are generally purchased about Christmas time, when the family has its annual settlement with the planter. They are bought in the nearby town, for cash, and though slightly better than the rest of the house would justify are not really an extravagance, since they consume only a part of the annual profits. The rest is spent for a grand debauch, lasting from two days to a week.

The plantation negro seems to have a weakness for a big wooden bed, " Wagner pants," a fashionable hat, and a yellow dog. Beyond these possessions, his sentiments and desires are entirely capricious. On Sundays and in the evenings most of the family spend their time on the gallery, talking, laughing in the loudest of voices, and exchanging plantation wit,—which is really sometimes funny,—with their callers, who seldom come into the house or even upon the gallery, but generally stand outside to talk to the family within. On most plantations the negro cabins are huddled together along the main road. Few of the negroes will consent to be put down into the middle of a square section of forty acres they may have leased. They declare it is " too lonesome "; and so the cabins which were once placed in that way have had to be moved up to the main road, and the little leaseholds have been changed into narrow strips. The negro is a gregarious animal, and he has absolutely refused to live in any way except with an abundance of next-door neighbours.

From his own point of view the plantation darkey

is certainly "living easy," as he himself calls it.
There is never any very cold weather, and there is
an abundance to eat for every one.    Any able-
bodied negro man can have for the asking as many
acres of land as he can possibly cultivate.    He will
be given a house free, and allowed for his own
use a plot of garden ground.    He will be furnished
with all his implements and given the use of a mule
to cultivate his little leasehold.    He has the use of
a plantation mule and wagon to haul his supply of
fuel, and the overseer will probably have to make
him do the hauling before the cold weather comes.
With a garden and free fuel, an energetic negro
can keep the wolf from the door, if he worked at
nothing else, but in return for his work in the field
he is paid in cash twenty-five cents per day, or is
allowed, at his option, half of the crop.    Practically
the only rations he draws from the plantation are
salt meat, tobacco, and salt.    These are deducted
from his wages, of course, but they do not form
a very large item, because the negro will not eat
fresh meat, as a rule, and very little of it even when
salted.

Out in the country beyond Indianola, Mississippi,
I made the acquaintance of the rural negro at work.
He is not a particularly desirable friend, and he
has learned by bitter experience that few white
men care to be friends with him.    His conversation
is in its own way strictly Biblical, being confined

for the most part to " Yes, boss," and " No, boss."
These negroes in the field do not look downtrodden
or abused. On the whole, they were dressed for
their work about as well as the average farm labourer in the North. The presence of women in
the cotton fields adds a picturesqueness to the country which one misses in the North, because the coloured women relieve the blackness of their faces by
the radiance of their attire, and there is none so
poor as not to have an effective turban or a brilliant
apron.

The most casual contact with the negro in the
fields, however, demonstrates his immense inferiority to the foreign labourer of the Middle and Western States. He is not of the same class at all; and
aside from all political speculation, and from questions of abstract right or wrong, it must be admitted
that the Southern plantation negro must necessarily
be treated in a different way, politically and socially, from the foreign labourer of the North. The
negro in the fields and along the roadside is as good-
natured a peasant as the sun ever shone upon. He
is almost childishly happy; he is the best common
labourer in the world, certainly for so hot a climate;
he does not much care to vote. He makes an excellent labourer under supervision, but if left to
himself will idle the day away with tranquil com-
placency. He is densely, hopelessly, predominantly
ignorant—far more ignorant than the census figures

would lead one to suppose. According to the official returns, about one-third of the American negroes can neither read nor write. But as a matter of fact, when the questions of the census enumerators were answered, many negro families were put down as able to read and write, whereas in many cases the only one thus accomplished in the whole family was a child, whose gifts in that line were probably not more striking than those to be witnessed in the lowest grade of a city grammar school.

The illiteracy of the negro, however, cannot be compared to that of the most densely ignorant whites who come to the North as immigrants from Europe. The negroes have an ignorance all their own, entirely aside from their inability to read and write. It is the ignorance of childhood, of unadulterated barbarism, but not of savagery. Few of them know how old they are; they cannot remember things a few years back; their notions of the government are of the vaguest possible character; they make contracts with the white men without the slightest conception of their meaning, and they break those contracts whenever it is their inclination to do so. The ignorance of the field negroes is almost incomprehensible to the average Northern man. Yet they are not vicious; they are unmoral rather than immoral; and there is no doubt of their susceptibility to education and refinement. They are human in every respect, and their ignorance is not because of their race, but because they have never had an opportunity to learn anything at all, either from books, from their parents, or from close observation of white men. There is plenty of good raw material in the negro, though at present the plantation blacks are a threat to the community in which they exist just as any other large body of ignorance would be. In a county where not one per cent of the negroes have an ordinary common school education, even though they are not naturally vicious, they are so suspicious of the white man and so easily led by the few half-educated men of their own race, that there is a good deal of justification for the belief that unless their ignorance is alleviated by a far wider application of the public school system than the South has shown any disposition to adopt, the time must come when by mere force of numbers the black man will drive the white man out of the plantation districts, as he has already driven him out of the cotton country in Dallas County, Alabama.

It was in this same Yazoo delta of Mississippi, where the picturesque Sunflower County lies, and where there are three negroes to every white person, that the results of the outnumbering of whites by blacks were most apparent to me. In the rural districts, the proportion at the time of my visit was at least ten to one, while in some " beats," which is the Mississippi name for townships, the ratio runs up to a hundred to one. The marvellous growth of the negro population here is almost entirely due to emigration from other sections. The fertile bottomlands have become a sort of paradise for the negroes. A large part of the old wilderness has of late years been broken up into cotton plantations, whose richness is not exceeded by that of any other section, save the Sea Island cotton fields. The whole country is intersected by bayous, and the development of railroads has furnished an easy market. Cotton compresses and cotton-seed oil mills have gone up all over this country. The immediate result is the large inrush of negro population into the Yazoo delta, and a demand for plantation labour which has made necessary the importation of negroes from Alabama and Georgia.

This is the cause. Now for the effect. Situated as they are in an overwhelming sea of black men, their wives and children at the mercy of the good nature of the negro, the white people have fallen into the habit of going armed, and pistols are far too common. For example, I watched one day half a dozen young white men, idlers of the ordinary country village type, who drifted into the Indianola drug store. While they were amusing themselves with the usual rustic horse-play, I counted no less than four protuberances in hip pockets—coats are not worn in Indianola in the middle of the day. One of the young fellows reached into another

young man's pocket, withdrew from it a loaded revolver, and flourished it about in the drug store,
without either the bystanders or the proprietor see-
ing anything unusual in the proceeding, though in
any law-abiding Northern community the act would
have resulted in immediate arrest.

This habit of carrying pistols may be a necessary
protection to the life and property of the whites,
and it would not do much harm, perhaps, if they
were all conservative and temperate men of mature
age.   In point of fact, however, many young men
in the South who have not reached the age of discretion, and above all who are accustomed to the
use of strong beverages at certain times, either carry
pistols constantly, or at least own and keep weapons
in the house.   As a result, the negro, with his imitative tendency, has begun, as I have already said,
to carry his pistol, too.   This is merely the usual
result of the pistol-carrying habit, as will be recognized by any one who has studied conditions in the
far West during the earlier days.   If a few men
in a community begin to carry pistols, their power
for good or evil over their associates is increased
so enormously that the others are obliged to carry
pistols, too.   The inevitable result is that where all
men are armed there is no disparity between their
fighting qualities, and they are no better off than
if no one was armed.

Indianola is the town which years ago achieved

an unsavoury reputation as a " town without a post-
office." At that time the impression went abroad
that the white people of the town were lawless, and
wholly unjust to the negro. Yet as a matter of
fact, at the time of my visit the negroes passed
through the streets as unmolested as in other cities;
and I learned that the enforced resignation of the
negro post-mistress was not due to race prejudice.
It was but natural that the white population of the
place, which does fully ninety-five per cent of all the
business in the local post-office, should resent the
appointment to the position of a negro girl, solely
at the dictation of a Republican referee in Jackson.
Moreover, the negroes got into the habit of congre-
gating about the post-office, although not one of
them in a hundred had any business there, and white
women and children were frequently made the ob-
jects of unpleasant comment by the post-office
loungers. This seems a small thing to Northern
people, but in the South, where the prejudices of
the white people must be regarded, the constant and
daily annoyance to women and children is a factor
which even a great government might take into consideration.

Around the streets of Indianola the visitor is
likely to meet an unfortunate negro known as
" Will," whose case is a proof that the now almost
forgotten post-office affair was no evidence of bitter
feeling on the part of the whites toward their black

neighbours.  I could not discover that Will had any other name.  My informant, a well-to-do and communicative woman, said casually :

" I don't guess these niggers don't never have any more'n one name, nohow."

Be that as it may, while still a young man Will had both his arms caught in a cotton gin, so that they had to be amputated at the elbows.  When he had sufficiently recovered from the accident to get about the town, he went to the county supervisors and applied for some little charity.  They informed him they could do nothing for him under the law except send him to the county poor farm, a place of horrors, as poor farms always are, whether north or south of Mason and Dixon's line.  Poor Will looked the supervisor in the face, looked down at his mutilated arms, brightened up a bit, and with a flash of unwonted determination said, " Well, boss, I 'low I'd ruther starve.  I 'low I'll hustle round a li'l bit, an' see ef dar ain't nothin' a nigger widout no arms kin larn t' do."

So Will hustled round.  He learned to do marvellous things without any arms.  I saw him driving a horse down the street with the reins fastened in some mysterious way to his stumps of arms.  He can vault a fence, and he can pull a child's express-wagon after him, and withal is as good-natured as the day is long.  Will has become a wonder in the number of things he can do, and the town people, recognizing his determination and worth of character, rewarded him when the opportunity came. They drove Minnie Cox, the negro woman, out of the local post-office because she permitted idlers of her own race to congregate about her office; but, on the other hand, these same queer people of Indianola, bearing no apparent malice against the race, forthwith appointed Will, the negro without hands, to carry the mail from Heathman, three miles up the Southern Railroad, to which all letters for Indianola were directed. Will has a public occupation and is paid by voluntary contribution of the citizens. History seems to suggest a phase of Southern character which Northern students of the negro question would do well to study.

The salvation of the State of Mississippi, as of the other Southern States, rests in the education of its negroes. Yet at the time I was there a man was running for governor who, they told me, would be elected, on a platform which involved the division of the State school fund, thus leaving the negro to provide for his own education. Such a plan means fewer schools for the negroes and more pistols for the whites, until in the fulness of time Mississippi shall become all black and all ignorant. It is a short-sighted policy at best, but the school problem in the South is something which requires more than casual study.

# A STUDY OF EXISTING
# CONDITIONS

# I

## The Economic Problem in the Black Belt

THE word "peonage" would be understood by few of the planters and by none of the negroes of the black belt of Georgia, Alabama, and Mississippi; yet the thing itself exists all about them. Involuntary servitude, always of black men to white masters, has long been the rule, not only in these States but in almost every strictly agricultural county throughout the real cotton belt. The planters and the negroes call it by very different names, but the involuntary servitude exists none the less, accompanied in many painful instances not only by restraint of the liberty of the individual, but by personal violence and by the degradation of the lash. Though investigations have been set on foot of late years, and efforts made to correct by law some of the most flagrant evils, nevertheless a barbarous system has grown up under cover of the authority of the State law, but in open defiance of the constitution of the United States. Contract labour laws which sanction imprisonment for debt and permit the involuntary servitude of human beings are most certainly unconstitutional.

Ask the most honest planter whether legalized slavery exists in his section. He would probably deny it, and his denial would be frank enough, from his point of view. He would explain the conditions on his own plantation by declaring that he merely enforced discipline, held his negro labourers to the performance of their contracts, and in other directions acted strictly under the State laws, without which, he would tell you, it would be impossible either to control the negroes or to operate the plantation. Yet at the same time the slightest investigation will establish the fact that whenever one gets away from the larger towns, the railroad stations, and the telegraph offices, the negroes on all the large plantations operated by white men, and in some cases on those managed by negroes themselves, are slaves in everything but name.

There are miles upon miles of the best cotton country in the world where the black people are subjected to " discipline " so severe, so brutal, and so effective that they are compelled to do exactly as the owner of the plantation orders them to do. Nominally they are free, but actually they are slaves. They cannot leave the plantation and go to work elsewhere; they cannot board a railroad train without permission; they cannot decide for themselves whether they are too sick to work or not; and, in many cases, refusal to work, running away, and similar offences, which in the North are considered as the most ordinary privileges of a free man, are punished with the lash or the buggy trace, which seems to be the favourite machine for producing "discipline."

There are almost as many phases of this twentieth-century slavery as there are of the negro question itself. In different communities throughout the black belt different devices are resorted to, which depend largely upon the character of the white population, although in each case, whatever the method, the disastrous result to the negro is practically the same. "Peonage" has been generally taken to mean the creation of a condition of legal slavery as a result of a conviction for crime, without subjecting the offender to confinement in a convict camp. This trick is resorted to largely, if not entirely, by the meanest, the most unscrupulous white classes of the South. It is the "pore white trash," the old overseer element, which resorts to this disreputable method under colour of law, but generally in violation of the State statutes themselves.

As conditions were at the time of my investigations, the method worked somewhat as follows: The negro would be charged by the white man with some insignificant offence, and fined an amount, enormous out of all proportion to the crime. Or, by a still better trick, the negro would be charged with having made threats of violence, and put under bond by a too friendly magistrate. Then the white

man, who had really provoked the entire prosecu-
tion, would step in and offer to go on the negro's
bond or to pay his fine.  In such a case the de-
fendant would hire himself out to the payer of the
fine, the contract being made in the open court so
as to have the approval of the magistrate.  Under
such a contract, the man who paid the fine or who
assumed the bond could hold the labourer in his employ until the debt thus created and acknowledged
in open court was satisfied.

Of course, there might be times when such a proceeding would be entirely humane, and when the
negro would gladly resort to it to escape the terrors
of a convict camp.  But it is obvious that even when
such a system is honestly administered, and the scant
safeguards the law has thrown about it are fully
observed, the ignorant negro, who can neither read
nor write, who has no roof over his head, no food
to put into his mouth, and no ballot to redress his
wrongs, invariably gets the worst of it.  The " pore
white trash " element, however, are not satisfied
with this large gamblers' percentage, and so have
gone outside of and beyond the law.  Having secured the negro as a contract labourer, they have
interpreted the law to mean that every subsequent
advance to the negro in cash or goods is part of
the original contract, and must be worked out by
involuntary servitude in the same way.  Furthermore, a custom has grown up of making these con-

tracts entirely outside the court, so that the negro has not even the protection of a white magistrate.

Trumped-up charges and collusion with unscrupulous justices, combined with an unfair and unmanly trading upon the gross ignorance of the negro, have resulted in transferring many of the black men into actual and, as they believe, perfectly legal slavery, which they have chosen in preference to the admitted misery of a convict's life.   This kind of peonage is chiefly built up on fraud, violence, and misrepresentation.   There is a second sort of peonage, however, which has grown up through no unfair application of the criminal law, but under the regular contract labour law which at the time of which I write was in force in Georgia and Alabama.

Throughout all the rural cotton counties of those States and others, the system of contracts for labour has long been used by large white planters and many negro planters as well.   Under the contract labour law, the planter makes written agreements with as many labourers as he may need.   These contracts are generally signed immediately after the holidays, and run, as a rule, until after the cotton is " set aside," which is the ordinary expression for the conclusion of the period of cultivation.   Now, if at the most only one-third of the negroes in America can read and write, it is obvious that these ignorant plantation negroes are hardly equipped to sign their names. They sign the contract as people sign an election petition in long rows below a printed, or, more often, a badly written caption at the top of the sheet—a caption which they cannot read. The signing takes place in the plantation office, under the oversight of the foreman or the owner himself. The negro, when his name is called, steps up and affixes his mark opposite what he is told is his name. No human being could ever recognize that mark, least of all could the negro himself identify it. In his gross ignorance he is at the mercy of the employer.

In course of time, however, the planters found that the negro invariably ran away, when he saw that he was unable to draw from the plantation a larger sum of money and goods than that to which his contract up to a given time had entitled him. They thereupon secured action by the legislature, enabling any planter to force the contract labourer to fulfil the terms of his agreement to the bitter end. To protect the planter, what was originally a mere civil contract became a virtual imprisonment for debt, with the right given to the planter to use force to make the labourer work from January until August, or for any other agreed time. The object of this law was not only to secure to the planter the return of money advanced in excess of the amount earned; its larger intent was to secure to him the right to make use of the labourer and to control the person of the labourer to the same extent when no advances at all had been made.

So unjust a measure could not remain in force unchallenged. After about two years it was declared unconstitutional by Judge Thomas G. Jones of Alabama. And quite in harmony with this declaration was the charge made to the Federal Grand Jury by Judge Emory Speer of Georgia to investigate the system of peonage, an utterance called forth by the arrest of three young planters in Jasper County, Georgia. The prosecutor in the case was a negro, who alleged that he had been held in actual slavery. He had made a contract to work for one of these men from January until August, and, like all negroes, had obtained one advance of money and rations after another. All of a sudden he found himself in debt for thirty-five dollars beyond the full amount of his contract, and thereupon, according to the usual negro custom, skipped out of the plantation during the night and went to work for another planter, a dozen or so miles away. He was, of course, traced there; and his employer, with another man, drove after him in a buggy, tied him to the back axle, and carried him back at full speed; the negro was dragged a part of the way and whipped incessantly, both en route and on arrival at the old plantation. The negro's wife managed to get down to Macon, where she swore out the necessary warrants to secure his release and the arrest of his captors.

The decisions of two such prominent judges of course went far toward modifying the abuses of the contract labour system. This fact meant much for the liberty of the negro; for while in the hands of honest, conscientious men this peonage did not work a great amount of harm to the negro, all owners were not honest, many of them were intemperate, all were prejudiced; and the right to reclaim a runaway labourer involves the use of an amount of force the measure of which is estimated by the white planter, and never by the ignorant, unfortunate negro.

It may be that there was no loss of life in executing this inhumane and outrageous contract labour law; and yet that is almost beyond belief; for the brutality and the passion which could enable one to whip a cowering negro might easily be carried to a greater extreme, and an old " nigger " more or less on a big plantation would hardly be a matter of comment.

Whatever improvement there may have been in conditions during the last few years, peonage certainly was in existence not many years ago, for in southwestern Georgia, in Sumter County, I saw and studied it in operation. This locality is in the heart of the black belt and of the cotton country, and is sufficiently removed from ordinary centres of trade to present the negro problem in its best and its worst phases. The peonage which I saw here was in such modified form as to be openly defended by prosperous and liberal planters, who, though they admitted the illegality, the brutality, and the downright wickedness of the system, yet declared it to be an economic necessity, owing to the fact that in this section the negroes outnumbered the whites three or four to one, and the well-educated whites fully ten to one.

Before giving the testimony of an honest but necessarily anonymous witness, it is only fair to both sides to explain briefly the relations between the two races as regards population and property interests.   There were in Sumter County at the time of my visit about 7,500 whites to 19,000 negroes.   Of the farms of the county, about half were in pieces of fifty acres or less, and no less than seventy-five were plantations ranging from five hundred to several thousand acres apiece.   Almost five hundred of the plantations were actually operated by the owners themselves, and embraced the greatest part of the cotton land of the section.   Around these five hundred white planters spread a negro population of nineteen thousand.   Bearing in mind these facts, it will be possible to appreciate the viewpoint of the white planter, expressed to me at first hand by a young man bearing a name famous in America.

This young planter was born in the South, educated at Columbia University, had five years of good business training in the North, and was then suddenly called home by the death of his father. Since then he had managed the plantation, with whose methods he had been familiar from childhood. What he told me would shock a great many people, and yet he told it with entire frankness, fully appreciating my own mission, but believing implicitly that the severe methods of government he had adopted were absolutely necessary for the protection of his life and property.

"When my father came down into the heart of the cotton belt," said this intelligent and engaging young planter, who had all a Northern man's energy and all a Southern man's delicacy and courtesy, "this section was just recovering from the war. It was during the reconstruction period and the negroes were on top. He had not been in charge of the plantation for more than twenty-four hours when a big salt-water negro came riding up on a mule, armed with a double-barrelled shotgun. He made no bones of his errand, but hunting up my father, covered him with the shotgun. 'White man,' he said, ' I'll give you just thirty minutes to get off this plantation; if you stay here after that time, I'll blow your head off.'

"This was the kind of treatment which had

driven every other white man off that plantation for a year or two.

"Fortunately, my father managed to decoy the negro off his mule, and engaged him in conversation until they were in the vicinity of a brush heap where his own gun lay. One barrel was loaded with buck shot for actual defence, the other barrel with split peas. Before that salt-water nigger knew what had happened to him, he got a dose from the left-hand, or split-pea barrel. It made quite a bit of a hole in the darkey's neck, but he never gave any more trouble from that day, and he is one of the old-time, stand-by darkies on the plantation at this minute."

Remembering that this incident was merely one of many similar cases in the horrible times of reconstruction and carpet-bag dominion, I was about to dismiss the subject, when my young friend began of his own accord to give me some instances of his own discipline, which, as he said, was that practised on every successful plantation in south-western Georgia. He said: "When the bell rings I expect all my people to start for the field. Promptness and punctuality in beginning work are just as essential in a cotton field in Georgia as in a cotton mill in Massachusetts, and five minutes delay by five hundred hands means a loss of about four days' time of a single man. It is this which counts. Supposing a woman were behind the others every day five, ten, or twenty minutes, and you had repeatedly remonstrated with her without effect, the woman seeming to take pride in showing her independence of you, what would you do with her?"

"I suppose I would have to let her go, and discharge her from my employ," I said.

"Oh, you would, would you? Well, suppose she had, as most of them have, about fifteen brothers and sisters, all married and most of them with children, so that the family connection amounted to from thirty to sixty persons. Now, if all were free agents, and that woman were discharged, every one of those people would skip with her. Half a dozen such cases of discipline would paralyze the plantation."

I readily admitted the economic problem, but innocently asked, "What did you do about it?"

"I'll tell you what I did. I stopped that woman just as she was coming out of the door, after all the other people had gone, and I said to her: 'Mirandy, blankety blank your blank black hide, if you're late again to-morrow I'll take you into the plough house, and I'll lay you out with the buggy trace so you'll stay laid for a good many days to come.'"

"But you never did whip a negro, of course?" I said.

"Yes, I have. We have to do it once in a while. A negro ran away from me and hid on the next plantation eleven miles away.  I went after him with my negro foreman.  I took him out of a cabin with a revolver in my hand and drove him home.  There I took it out of him with the buggy whip, while the negro foreman held him.

" That sounds shocking to you, no doubt, but I am telling you the fact.  If you were the only responsible white man on a plantation, and were surrounded by more than five hundred negroes of the most debased and ignorant character, who cannot be reached by any moral suasion, who are influenced by neither gratitude nor resentment, you would go to the field every day with a revolver in your pocket, just as every one of us planters is forced to do; and you would either maintain discipline in the only way the negro understands, or else you would give up your plantation to your creditors, or your executors, as the case might be."

" Running away " is a recognized offence in this section.  Just what peonage consists of here I will let my young planter friend explain in his own words.

" We have two ways of handling our plantations," he said.  " We rent small sections of forty acres each, and with these go a plough and a mule. You know it is figured out that a mule can cultivate forty acres of cotton.  In addition to that, however, I have about 450 hands who work on wages. These men are paid nine dollars a month, in addition to a fixed ration of food, which amounts to four pounds of meat a week, a certain percentage of vegetables, tobacco, sugar, flour, and some other commodities. The cash wages used to be eight dollars in addition to the rations, but the price has risen, owing to the high rates for cotton.

" These negroes live on the plantation, are given a roof over their head, have garden patches, and several other more or less valuable privileges. They invariably come to me for small advances of money. I have to keep a ledger account with every negro on the plantation. If a man has a large family, his ration, of course, is not sufficient and he has to draw more, the actual cost to be deducted from his cash wages.

" No negro on my plantation has ever charged me with getting him into debt or with failing to pay him the entire sum stipulated in his contract. They all make contracts with us individually. Not one in ten can sign his name, but I write out the names and each negro in my employ puts his mark there in the presence of negro witnesses. The terms of the contract are never in dispute, and it is a matter of pride with most of us white men that no living person shall be able to say we have taken advantage of our negroes.

" Now, when a negro runs away and violates his contract, leaving us in the lurch, not only short of his labour, but short of the advances we have made

to him in money and goods, what would happen if
we depended simply and solely upon our right to
sue? In the first place, with 450 hands, before the
season is out we would have 450 suits, and if we
won them all we would not be able to collect forty-
five cents, because it is literally true that the field
labourer has nothing in this world except the clothes
on his back, and he doesn't always have too many
of them. The result is that in Georgia and Alabama and, I believe, in other States, the law recognizes the right of the planter to reclaim the labourer who has left in violation of his contract,
whether he be actually in debt or not.

" Under any other system you would find it impossible to get in your cotton, because the negroes
at the critical time would simply sit down and refuse
to work. When they are well we compel our labourers to go to the field by force. This is the
truth, and there is no use in lying about it."

These are but fragments of a conversation which
seems clearly to establish the fact that in most of
the big cotton plantations in the South the negro
is held to labour under a contract. This contract
is renewable yearly, and at the date when it is renewable the negro is free to leave the plantation, as
he frequently does, although he does not generally
go outside a radius of a dozen miles.

The conversation shows also that the cotton
planters, acting under colour of State laws which

have now been declared unconstitutional, have assumed the right to force the negro labourer to live up to the terms of his contract, and to reclaim him when he runs away; and that in extreme cases the buggy whip and the buggy trace are resorted to, to enforce discipline.

There is a still deeper and more painful inference from the conversation, growing out of the fact that nearly every planter, or at least every white overseer, goes to the cotton field on horseback armed. It is not too much to suppose that there are not some negroes who will resist the application of force with such force of their own as God has put into their athletic black-skinned bodies. So the inference is painfully apparent that the white man on the horse with the pistol in his pocket is now and then compelled to use it. Often, perhaps, the compulsion to use the pistol is more apparent to him than to the negro.

I give these facts without comment, as to whether the economic necessity justifies the disregard of the moral law or not. However that may be, these are the facts, sad though they be.

## II

## Where the White Planter Is the Negro's Friend

THERE is at least one Southern gentleman who has not used the contract labour system in managing his plantation. This is Mr. J. Adger Smyth, for years the broad-minded and effective mayor of Charleston. His experience in managing a plantation at once for the good of his labourers and for his own profit is an interesting example of the economic problem as complicated by the negro question.

When the war closed, Mr. Smyth found himself the proprietor of a plantation with two hundred and fifty slaves. He marshalled them before the big house, and there, like many another slaveholder throughout the South, read to them Lincoln's Emancipation Proclamation, and told them they were free to go where they wished.

Following upon this interesting sermon, Mr. Smyth was at once confronted with the problem of how to keep his negroes from starving. He had no money; the land was exhausted; the coloured people were hungry, and in spite of the Emancipation Proclamation, still looked to him for food and clothes. Securing the services of a Yankee sergeant from a nearby military post, to guarantee the honesty of his proposition, Mr. Smyth agreed to farm the whole plantation on shares.  The owner supplied the land, furnished the seed, the agricultural implements, the mules, the cabins in which the coloured people lived, and every other possible accessory. He had no money, but he had credit, and thus was enabled to put the negroes in the way to earn their own living.  He took two-thirds of the receipts and the negroes one-third.  In this way the negro labourer received one-third of the gross value of the product of his labour, entirely independent of other expenses, a ratio of wages which, in theory at least, is abundantly liberal.

The outcome of this experiment might well be told by Mr. Smyth himself.

" At the end of four years," he said, " I found myself $10,000 in debt on the plantation, and as I had no means, I determined to cut loose then and there.  I drew up a sort of proclamation as nearly as possible in official form, called the darkies up to the big house again, just as I had done four years before, and told them that this was *my* emancipation proclamation, which had freed me after all.  I took a mighty oath then and there I would never raise another bale of cotton on my own hook, and I never have.

"I then began a new scheme. I rented the land outright at two dollars an acre, and have continued this practice ever since. I gave them free, of course, all their cabins and the usual gardens about them, and made repairs on houses and fences about the plantation. Out of from four thousand to five thousand acres, I could rent until recently only three hundred acres, but this year this amount has greatly increased, and I shall be able to have about one thousand acres under lease."

This experience seems largely to corroborate the testimony of the planter quoted in the last chapter, to the effect that a plantation can hardly be managed in an altruistic spirit and at the same time produce profits. So also does the story of the experience of Mr. Stone of Greenville, before alluded to, who has been the victim to a certain extent of a philanthropic experiment he made for the benefit of the negroes of his own plantation, and who nevertheless discusses more dispassionately than most Southerners the question of the economic and industrial relations of the negro.

"I tried to force my negro tenants," he said in telling his story, "to save some money in spite of themselves. I made them the most liberal kind of terms, and put the whole transaction on a strictly business basis, although my motives were entirely in the direction of helping the negroes. I gave them one, two, and even three years' time in which to

purchase a mule and the necessary farm implements.
I held them down on all advances of provisions and
supplies, and did my best to force them to become
independent. I am sorry to say that the effort has
not been successful. I have divided up sixty-seven
small pieces of land, and in each case made such
terms as would enable the tenant with ordinary in-
dustry to buy his own mule and the necessary farming implements, so as to render him independent of
the owner of the soil except for the ordinary ground
rent.

" We make our new arrangements with the coloured people along about the holidays, and last
Christmas no less than seventeen families which I
had helped to become independent no sooner found
themselves with a mule and a little property paid
for, than they left the plantation and forced me to
seek new tenants and go through the same long
operation again. They were induced to leave and
to go to work on a nearby plantation which had
previously been worked by convict labour, now being withdrawn to the State camps.

" These negro tenants left without any effort on
their part to examine into their new farms, and
found when it was too late that they were expected
to live in huts which would not keep out the rain
and were not supplied with any of the comforts to
which they had been accustomed. They had a perfect right to go away, but it seemed at least ungrate-

ful to leave the planter who had helped them to
independence without the slightest compunction.
This is generally the result of almost every effort
honestly made by humane planters for the betterment of the negro."

Such a report is discouraging.  Verily, it is hard
to choose between the two horns of the dilemma.
It is a question for the individual conscience to decide, whether to reap what profits can be reaped
from the use of force and the consequent degradation of the negro, or to sacrifice the profits in the
somewhat chimerical hope of improving the negro's
condition.  That improvement would appear to be
a matter for the far future, even in the hands of
the most scrupulously humane employers; yet surely
the planters who enforce their contract labour system by means of whip and pistol are not aiding
greatly in the ultimate solution of the race problem
in America.  It is once more a choice between the
individual and the public good—the public being in
this case not the negro, but the South itself.

Anomalous as it may seem, this Yazoo delta country in Mississippi has a greater scarcity of labour
than the States of Georgia and Alabama, where contract labour and harder conditions are the rule.  In
order to supply the demand for labour in this fertile cotton country, where it brings a higher price
than almost anywhere else, the planters have been
compelled to send to neighbouring States for their

negroes. In Georgia and Alabama a license tax of some five hundred dollars is imposed in each county for agents who seek to send negroes out of the State. When the tenants and field hands drift away from Mississippi, now that the cotton area has been increased so largely, the planters are forced to send to the nearby States and to pay the excessive rates by which Alabama and Georgia are seeking to stop the drain upon their negro population.

The outnumbering of the whites by the blacks is not an ideal condition of things; yet it is a curious fact in the South that wherever the black men are in the greatest majority they appear to be the most docile. Tensas Parish, the garden spot of Louisiana, is a complete and unimpeachable proof of this peculiar condition. This section, where the town of St. Joseph is situated, is the heart of the black belt of the State. The parish has about fifteen times as many negroes as whites, yet a serious clash between the races is rarely heard of, the crime of all crimes, which is supposed to justify lynching, is equally unknown, and the relations between the two races, while essentially those of slavery days, are cordial, kindly, and sympathetic.

The tropical conditions here make the country a paradise for the negro. The climate is about what he is accustomed to; the vegetation is luxuriant; a living can be had from the generous soil with the minimum of labour; and there are abundant oppor-

tunities for the idle darkey to bask in the sun, like
the alligator in the nearby swamp.  Around about
are the pecan trees and the great blossoms of the
magnolia; the rich blooms of the crepe myrtle and
the mimosa tree; the live oak and the cottonwood
with its blowing fleece.  In the lakes one can find
with the simplest hook and line the " Sac au Lait,"
which is the Creole name for the white bass; while
spread over the surface of the swamp are millions
and millions of the " Monokonut," or sacred yellow
lotus.  The alligator is still to be found in the more
remote pools, although the rifle quickly exterminates
the reptiles in the more accessible lakes and bayous.
On the galleries of the plantation houses one can
find the nest of the mocking-bird, and hear him
singing his most marvellous song on moonlight
nights, while the bobolink, the cardinal bird, and
myriads of the most beautiful humming-birds are
seen at every moment.

It is all so tropical and so beautiful that one
realizes why the negro is so contented here,—since
he is indifferent to the drawbacks of the climate—
the mosquitoes, the miasma of the swamps, the de-
pressing moist heat, and the swamp water, which
produces all sorts of disorders among civilized white
men.  The vines which cover all the trees, the
festoons of Spanish moss, all the extravagant lux-
uriance of the tropical vegetation appeal to the negro as nothing else can, satisfying his hereditary

tastes, teaching that a living is to be had with little effort, and thus making him what he undoubtedly is to-day—hopelessly ignorant and debased, but none the less absolutely peaceable, tractable, contented, and happy.

Tensas Parish is essentially a community of the few rich and the many poor. There is neither poverty among the whites nor wealth among the negroes. There are a few white planters and thousands upon thousands of negro labourers. The relative proportion as between the ruling class of whites and the ruled class of blacks has been altered but little in the last thirty years. The town of St. Joseph is made up of the residences of cultivated, prosperous white planters, who have gradually given up the old system of living in isolation on their own plantations, and have gathered here along the river-banks. Living in this way, they are in connection by steamer with Natchez and Vicksburg, and can have ice and other such civilized necessities landed at their own doors. More than that, living as neighbours, they secure the society of people of their own class. Every one in town is either a planter or indirectly interested in a plantation; so whenever a knot of men gathers on a corner, their conversation inevitably turns to the question of the prospect of rain or sun, schemes for the destruction of the boll weevil, and similar topics of high importance on the plantations.

The whole country hereabouts is below the high water level of the Mississippi, and it is only the great levee stretching along the banks of the river which guards and protects the plantations. All this section of Louisiana was once under the sea, and it is scarcely out of it yet. The soil is as rich as anything in the world, not excepting the famous delta of the Nile, because it is made up of the drainings of the entire Mississippi valley. No one knows the depth of this silt, which will grow the most marvellous crops year after year without fertilizing. A cotton crop is occasionally succeeded by one of corn with peas sown between the rows, it having been found that peas are amply sufficient to restore in a single season everything that the cotton has taken away from the composition of the soil.

These physical conditions bring about a state of affairs which is ideal for the negro, but which at the same time renders the planter almost absolutely dependent upon black labour. There is here not the slightest reason in the world why any black man of good health should fail to support his family with absolute abundance. Northern friends of the negro would do well to study this statement in all its bearings. It is not extravagant to say that it would be difficult to find an able-bodied man or woman in Tensas Parish who has not at his command the means of making a livelihood much better than that granted to the average white immigrant in any Northern State. This does not mean that the condition of the negro, mentally and morally, is not shocking. But so far as conditions in Tensas Parish can be considered at all typical, Northern philanthropy should be extremely cautious before it disturbs an economic situation which is so extremely satisfactory to the negro himself. Great care must be exercised that in endeavouring to better his condition it may not be made worse.

The demand for agricultural labour in this section is almost unlimited. Thousands of acres of fertile land are yet awaiting development, and the labour supply is not sufficient to take care of the land already under cultivation. As a result, the negro can command a good wage for his labour, paid in almost any form he likes. Any negro who wants it will be given as large a farm as he desires, for which he can pay rent in cash, or part in cash and part in crops, or all in crops. He can rent out his own labour for a cash payment per day or for part cash, and in either of these cases he will be guaranteed a roof over his head and other comforts which make his living absolutely secure. This is not an overdrawn picture, nor is it a presentation of the white man's side of the situation. It is an absolute fact that any able-bodied negro can readily earn enough to put by money every year, if he can be taught habits of thrift and of foresight.

Supposing a negro determines to become a tenant

farmer.    Every white man in the vicinity will be
glad to get him and he will be given his choice of
terms.    That is to say, a negro who has not a dollar
in the world, who has nothing at his command beside his strong hands and his tropical, anti-malarial
constitution, will be given first of all the exclusive
control of, say, forty acres of land, if he can handle
that much.    He will be given the use, free of charge,
of a mule, a plough, and all necessary farming implements.    While he remains on his little farm he
will have assigned to him a one-story, one-roomed
house for his own use and that of his family.    Attached to that will be as large a garden patch as
he desires to cultivate during his leisure hours.    In
the vicinity is an abundance of wood, belonging to
the plantation, which he can have for his own use,
and which will cost him only the trouble of cutting
it down and hauling to his cabin door.    The plantation will supply the axe for the former and a mule
and team for the latter.    He will be given absolute
permission to keep a cow and as many chickens and
pigs as he may desire.    All the proceeds of his garden patch, of his pigs, his chickens, and his cow
are his own, and the demand for such products in
the plantation settlement among the " white folks "
with their big, fine houses always exceeds the
supply.

All this is what the white man gives the negro.
In return the negro gives absolutely nothing at all

but the labour of his hands. When the crop of
cotton is safely ginned it is divided, one-half going
to the owner of the soil and one-half to the negro.
If the labourer prefers, he can receive wages paid
to him in cash. That is to say, the planter will supply the land, the house, the fuel, the garden patch,
the mule, and the plough, and will take his chances
on the crop, paying the negro in cash every two
weeks seventy-five cents per working day, and sixty
cents for his wife or his full-grown daughter, if
they choose to work in the field.

If a negro labourer desires to avoid all other re-
sponsibilities, he can secure ordinary day labour in
the cotton and the corn, and receive $1.25 a day.
When one studies these figures it is impossible to
escape the conclusion that the ordinary, ignorant,
improvident, and naturally idle negro labourer is
immeasurably better off in Tensas Parish than he
would be in some of the best agricultural sections
of the North. The planters are seeking to encourage tenant farming. They ask nothing from the
tenant but honest labour. Plantation stores are not
always good things, and they frequently sell liquor
to the negro when he should not have it, but on
the whole the agricultural labour in this section is
not tied down by unfair restrictions, nor is there
anything in the way of downright prosperity, except the inherent constitutional inability of the ignorant negro to look ahead.

Every pay day, those who receive cash wages go either to the plantation store, to some cross-roads gin-mill, or to the county town of St. Joseph, and there in an incredibly short time dispose of almost every penny of their hard-earned money. For this reason it will be seen that some sort of a credit system on the plantation is absolutely indispensable to the negro. To abolish it would mean beyond a doubt the starvation of the negro, since in his present state of mental development he cannot be trusted to look ahead a month or a week, many times not even a day. The average negro labourer on a plantation, if stocked up with meat enough to last him three months, will either eat it all, or waste it all, or sell it all, or gamble it all, or lose it all in some mysterious way, inside of the first few weeks, and then will beg for more. The only safety for this negro is to draw his rations from the smoke-house twice a week, and have them charged to his account.

The better class of planters is rapidly coming to the conclusion that it cannot cope with the characteristic improvidence of the negro until it removes whiskey altogether from his reach. This has been largely responsible for the rapid spread of prohibition sentiment in the Southern States. In Louisiana, this sentiment first found expression in a voluntary but concerted effort to stop the sale of whiskey in the plantation stores and confine it entirely to the larger towns, so as to make it difficult for the negroes to obtain it.

This negro dissipation is a serious matter for the planter.  There are times in the cultivation of the cotton crop when abundant labour and quick work are indispensable.  If at that particular time a large body of negroes sees fit to go off on a debauch, the planter is frequently the only loser.  Self-interest, therefore, has had a part in inducing the intelligent cotton planter to cultivate friendly relations with his black labour, not only by helping them to keep out of debt, but also by helping them at the same time to keep as far away as possible from the whiskey barrel, which to the negro, even more than to the Indian, is a racial calamity.  The Indian gets fighting drunk and then stops drinking for a while; but the plantation negro, if allowed to have his way, becomes a confirmed dipsomaniac, and can keep away from whiskey only when he has no money to buy it.

In the sugar-growing sections of Louisiana industrial conditions are very similar to those in the cotton country, except that here all the work is done by day labour.  There is no opportunity to establish a tenant system, since so much capital is involved in the raising and marketing of sugar cane. The labourer in the sugar fields is paid seventy-five cents a day, in the ordinary season, and his wife sixty cents, while in the busy season he receives at least $1.25 a day, with often seventy-five cents extra for half a night's work. Occasionally the prices run even higher. Besides the cash wage, the labourer has the same privileges as the cotton worker, as to house, fuel, stock, garden produce, and the use of the plantation implements.

I was told by Governor Sanders of the Louisiana contract labour law and its working. " We have neither credits nor contracts in the sugar country," he said. " We do not appeal to the contract labour law except in the busy harvest season, when we have to import hands by thousands from Alabama and pay their fare. Then we force them to stay on the plantation until they have at least worked out their railroad fare. None of our planters run stores any more. There is a store on each plantation, of course, but it is rented by a merchant. The planter does not assume to collect any debts for that merchant, although, as a matter of convenience, wages are paid at this store, where the plantation office is, and the merchant collects his debts then and there. We all pay cash, or what is equivalent to cash, and on some plantations the hands are paid every day, the overseer giving out plantation pay checks for the exact amount earned. These pay checks are redeemed in cash at least every few weeks, and they serve as currency, circulating over the parish, but seldom remaining unredeemed over the regular day.

" The prices in the plantation stores are not extravagant, since a supply of labour always available is actual capital to any sugar planter, and we cannot afford to have these plantation stores so managed that the negroes will leave us.  So when we find that the prices are too high, or that the negroes are encouraged to buy things they do not really need, or that they are allowed to run hopelessly in debt, we notify the merchant at once that he must get down to the legitimate method or we will rent the store to some one else.  The result is that the prices in our plantation stores are not materially higher than in the towns, except for the slight advance caused by the cost of hauling from the railroads, which is often a long distance, and for which the negroes would have to pay themselves if they dealt in the towns.  These conditions of abundance of work for the negroes, of fair wages, and of decent treatment, with cash payment, make our part of the State a paradise to the darkies, but what we are going to do when the old-time negro disappears, I must frankly say I do not know."

# III

## The Political Issue

THE hysteria in the North over the negro question is most often aroused by the political situation in the South. But with all its iniquities, with all its injustice to the black man, this same political situation is one which should not be rashly disturbed. " Go slow " is the best possible motto for the statesman both North and South, when dealing with any of the curious political aspects of the race question. Without denying that there is great opportunity for improvement, it is none the less true that the Northern enthusiast or the Southern conservative who assumes rashly to disturb existing political conditions in the South must perhaps take the responsibility of inflicting vast harm upon the entire country.

I doubt if there is a first-class hotel in any large Northern city which could make a practice of receiving negro guests and keep out of bankruptcy. Yet in these same Northern communities, where, very properly, the negro is not granted the slightest semblance of social equality, the demand is constantly made that the South shall permit him to vote and hold important offices, which would of necessity involve him in constant association with the white people.    The people of the North must divest themselves of the idea that the welfare of the negro is for the present at least in any way connected with the exercise of the right of suffrage.

The Mecca of the Southern negro to-day is Washington.    Why is this?    Neither negroes nor whites vote in the District of Columbia.    The white and black children are provided with separate schools, and the lines between the two races are drawn with a care entirely unknown in cities a few degrees farther north.    In New York or Chicago the negro can secure the unrestricted right of suffrage, and his children can sit side by side in the public schools with the boys and girls of white parents.    Yet the negro does not hurry North, not only because the avenues of employment are not as good there as in the South, but also because in the North he is treated as a man, and if he does not work is apt to starve.    Until the negroes gather in sufficient quantities in the North to make them an important political factor, their right of suffrage will not appear particularly valuable to them.    In the Middle States and those of the middle West, it is well known that the negroes generally sell their votes at every election, a statement that cannot be controverted by any well-informed, frank politician from either party.    On the other hand, in the South, which is governed exclusively by white men, my own observation has shown me that a cleaner state of politics exists than in the North. Vote buying is not common, and the average scale of political morality in the cotton States is decidedly high.

I do not believe any intelligent, fair-minded, and liberal Northern man can spend even a few months in an exclusive investigation of the race question without becoming convinced, as I have become convinced, that the granting of suffrage to the negroes, immediately after the war, was a horrible blunder. For while here and there one may find negroes who are eminently fitted to exercise the right of suffrage, the time has not yet come when it is safe to give the ballot to the illiterate negro millions. It is doubtless true that the methods adopted by the South to eliminate the negro from politics were at first generally cruel, and are now frequently unconstitutional, but an honest survey of the situation must prove that they adopted the only way to repair the serious breach in the social and commercial fabric of the South, and that the end justified the means.

There are educated negroes, thousands of them, not at all confined to college professors or philanthropists. The negro schools are continually turning out a class of educated black men and women who are born in America, who are acquiring property interests, and who have quite enough education to enable them to make an intelligent use of the ballot. It must be remembered none the less that the great mass of the negro population of the South, embracing many millions of men and women, is not only wholly unfitted to exercise the right of suffrage, but if given the ballot at this stage in their race history, would undoubtedly become a menace to the welfare of the nation. There is a vast deal of difference between Professor DuBois of Atlanta University and the half-savage labourer in the rice fields or the cotton islands on the Atlantic coast. The difficulty of the problem lies in the fact that for every Booker Washington there are about 500,000 debased and debasing negroes.

Roughly speaking, one-ninth of the population of the United States is made up of negroes of various degrees of blackness. In a large number of the counties and congressional districts of the Southern States they constitute, as we have seen, an actual majority of the population. The negro vote, if the suffrage were granted him in the South, and if his vote were cast solidly and counted honestly, would elect enough United States senators, in all probability, to become a balance of power in that body. The negro would also elect a large percentage of the Southern members of the House of Representatives. The result would be that all the property interests of the South would practically be disfranchised. Even without the evils of " carpet-bagism," it is easy to figure out that within a few years after the application of an unqualified manhood suffrage for the negroes, they would control the Southern States, politically, socially, and morally, and would either destroy the cultured, wealthy white class or drive it northward.

The existence of such busy commercial and industrial centres as Atlanta and Birmingham is absolutely dependent upon the brains, the energy, and the capital of the white man. Withdraw these, and the cotton mill, the blast furnace, and even the fields of cotton, cane, and corn would have to be abandoned. The negro as a race in America is hundreds of years ahead of his brother in Africa; but though that is much to his credit, it does not alter the fact that he is thousands of years behind his white neighbour.

Look, for example, at the case of Charleston, the home of a cultured aristocracy; the home, also, of several thousand more negroes than whites. It is readily seen why the white people of Charleston insist upon keeping a tight rein upon the city government. A general election with a full count and a free ballot would, as a matter of course, fill every office in the city of Charleston with a negro, and thus would be reproduced the intolerable condition of the reconstruction period. Two alternatives only were open to the white population of such a city. They must either themselves seize and hold the government, at all hazards; or they must leave the city, abandoning it to negro domination. And in the latter case, white capital and business incentive being removed, the negro would starve to death.

This is the problem which is being worked out in the South; and while it is undeniably true that the negro is absolutely deprived of the franchise, it is also true that the white man treats him with great fairness and forbearance, and that putting aside the abstract question of right and wrong, the negro is far better off in Charleston to-day than he was when he had the ballot, and by its exercise precipitated the reign of terror that in those days prevailed.

It is a simple thing to stand in a Northern pulpit or to sit in a Northern office chair and from that safe vantage ground to speak or write about equal rights, the genius of the American Constitution, the beauty of a free ballot; but the political situation in the South is not a matter of theory, but of fact. If it happens to come in conflict with our American institutions, so much the worse for the institutions. Looked at from the standpoint of theory, the existing political situation in all the Southern States is a cruel outrage, a manifest violation of the basic principles of the Declaration of Independence; looked at in the light of social, commercial, and moral conditions, it is evident that to disturb present conditions rashly, in obedience to the voice of uninformed Northern demagogues, would be disastrous, first to the white man, but ultimately and most completely to the black man.

To travel through the South is to become constantly more and more impressed with the fact that the best interests of the negro are not in any way identified with politics. Whether he has or has not the ballot is a matter which may well be left for settlement until his material and intellectual condition has been vastly improved. For what the negro most needs to-day is education of head and hand, an education whose sole object shall be to help him earn his daily bread, to teach him to dispose intelligently of the fruits of his labour. Give the ballot to-day to the tens of thousands of ignorant negroes in the cane fields of Louisiana, and they will be much worse off in a year's time than they now are. The ballot would not procure them another day's work, nor would it better their social condition, because they could not apply the right of suffrage intelligently. That is to say, the negro as a whole, no matter how he may be mistreated and imposed upon by the white people, cannot better his condition by going into the voting booth, because he cannot apply the remedy of the ballot in such a way as to create a change for the better.

I have listened to some terrible stories of the reconstruction period. I have talked to some successful Northern men, now living in the South, who have themselves told me that no one can comprehend the horrors of that period, except those who have lived through it. Most of the evils of the carpet-bag era grew out of the dense ignorance of the negroes themselves. I have seen orders of court to which was attached a cross, witnessing the signature of a negro circuit judge who could neither read nor write, and who nevertheless held in his hands by law the power of life and death and of the distribution of property.

It will be many a year before the Southern negro can be educated up to a point where he can be trusted to discriminate between right and wrong, between good men and bad men, so far as the suffrage is concerned. Just at the present time, the great masses of the negroes are densely ignorant; but they have their race prejudice, just as much as the white man, and when they have the ballot their votes will go to the negro candidate, never to the white man. The minute that the negro is given the ballot, whether he acts collectively or not, he has become an object of interest to the practical white politician; and no one who pretends to understand the negroes can escape the conviction that even if they were restricted to a ballot for white candidates, their votes would surely be given to the highest bidder. The negro in the South will not be fitted to exercise the right of suffrage until the percentage of illiteracy is enormously decreased, and this will take not decades, but generations.

While it is true that the Southern negro as a whole is not fitted to exercise the right of suffrage, it is equally true that the Southern white man has endeavoured to eliminate him by means of methods so unequal in their operation, so manifestly unfair, as to cause resentment on the part of the negro, leading the black man to believe that the laws made by the white man are no better than those he himself would enact. Most Southern public men freely admit this fact, but they point out that they are endeavouring to correct by means of local statutes the original monumental blunder which was committed when the negro, fresh from the debasing influences of slavery, was given the ballot.*

The weakness of the political situation in the South is the fact that the white leaders have been afraid to take hold of the problem honestly, that is to say, they have either been afraid or unable to enact laws which would apply equally to white and

* Amendments to Constitution, 1865-1870:

ARTICLE XIII. *Section 1.*—Neither slavery nor involuntary servitude, except as a punishment for crime whereof the party shall have been duly convicted, shall exist within the United States, or any place subject to their jurisdiction.

ARTICLE XIV. *Section 1.*—All persons born or naturalized in the United States and subject to the jurisdiction thereof, are citizens of the United States and of the State wherein they reside. No State shall make or enforce any law which black men. The safety of the South undoubtedly lies in a system of suffrage based upon the possession of property, or upon an educational qualification, or upon both. Nevertheless, one Southern legislature after another has passed laws which seemed to discriminate between white and black, and which, although they may be pronounced constitutional, are repugnant to the ordinary Anglo-Saxon sense of justice.

In Georgia there are no limitations on the suffrage either for black or for white men, so far as the statute books show. The negro can vote if he wants to, but he has stopped wanting to in Georgia, for two distinct reasons. In the first place the white men are united solidly, and there is practically only one party in the State, so that the negro finds it useless to cast his vote. Secondly, he discovers that the negro who mixes in politics frequently finds it difficult to secure work, and while not in fear of bodily violence, he knows that on the whole his life will be longer and freer from care if he refrains

shall abridge the privileges or immunities of citizens of the United States; nor shall any State deprive any person of life, liberty, or property, without due process of law; nor deny to any person within its jurisdiction the equal protection of the laws.

ARTICLE XV. *Section I.*—The right of citizens of the United States to vote shall not be denied or abridged by the United States or by any State on account of race, colour, or previous condition of servitude.

from the ballot-box habit entirely. In the other Southern States resort has been had to various devices, too numerous and complicated to describe here, but all based upon the same unfair and unequal principle of writing a law which on its face is applicable to all men alike, but which in fact allows the white man to vote, without regard to his disqualifications, but prevents the black man from voting, no matter how well fitted he may be to exercise the right of suffrage. For example, in Virginia the negro applicants for the privilege of voting have been required to write out and define such expressions from the constitution as " writ of supersedeas," " ex post facto," and " bill of attainder." It is safe to say that few white men except lawyers, even in the educated North, could give offhand a satisfactory definition of these three terms. This " understanding " clause * is the favourite device throughout the South. On its face it seems fair enough to require that an intending voter shall not only be able to read and write, but shall show his mental capacity by demonstrating that he understands what he reads or writes, thus proving

* ARTICLE II. *Section 19.*—Fourth: A person able to read any section of this Constitution submitted to him by the officers of the registration and to give a reasonable explanation of the same; or, if unable to read such section, able to understand and give a reasonable explanation thereof when read to him by the officers. (Virginia Constitution, 1902— Elective Franchise.)

that he is capable of applying the ballot in a proper manner. That is the theory of the situation; but of course every one knows that all the election clerks are white men, who see to it that no negroes are allowed to vote where there is the slightest danger of their controlling the local political situation. The whole power rests in the hands of these election officers. They can readily be satisfied that the white man understands a specified section of the constitution, but they can never be brought to admit that the would-be black voter comprehends what he reads or writes.

I saw hanging on the library wall in Booker Washington's home in Tuskegee his life certificate, which showed that he had passed the necessary examination and could always be permitted to vote, so far as educational qualifications are concerned, in the State of Alabama. On the other hand, I talked with an intelligent young coloured man in Virginia who could read and write, who was an accomplished bookkeeper, stenographer, typewriter, and journalist, and who had been refused the right of suffrage because he could not offhand give a satisfactory definition of a " writ of supersedeas." I saw at the same time one of the election judges who refused this man the right of suffrage. He was an ignorant, fat, half-drunken saloon keeper, manifestly without the slightest particle of education or social standing, and infinitely the inferior, physically, mentally, and morally, of the coloured man he turned away from the election booth.

The " grandfather " clause * in many of the States was merely a temporary expedient. It consisted in permitting any man to vote, who could show that his grandfather or father exercised the right of suffrage prior to or about the time of the Civil War. Such a legal device would be absurd in the North, where the communities rapidly change; but there are few or no immigrants in the Southern States, and families remain about the

---

* The equivalent of the following is adopted in the Constitutions of various Southern States, with relation to the provisions as to the elective franchise:

*North Carolina.*—" Every person presenting himself for registration shall be able to read and write any section of the Constitution in the English language; and before he shall be entitled to vote he shall have paid on or before the first day of May, of the year in which he proposes to vote, his poll-tax for the previous year, as prescribed by Article 5, Section 1, of the Constitution. *But no male person, who was, on January 1, 1867, or at any time prior thereto, entitled to vote under the laws of any State of the United States wherein he then resided, and no lineal descendant of any such person, shall be denied the right to register and vote at any election in this State, by reason of his failure to possess the educational qualifications herein prescribed. . . ."* (Revisal of 1905, North Carolina, Vol. 2, Art. 6, Sec. 4, Constitution of North Carolina.)

The effect of this is to make the registration of negro voters so difficult as to amount to a prohibition.

same, so that thousands of ignorant white men who could neither read nor write had no difficulty in tracing their ancestors to recognized citizens of the commonwealth, who had exercised the right of suffrage fifty years ago.

This of course enabled the ignorant white men to vote, while it disfranchised practically all the coloured men, as there were only a few free negroes prior to the war who had any rights to citizenship, and the difficulty of tracing their posterity is something well understood by Southern students of the race question.

The " grandfather " clause was born in Louisiana, and its father was the present governor of the State.  The scheme has been copied in one form or another by almost all the Southern States, but it is worthy of note that as originally devised in Louisiana it was applied with strict impartiality. Governor Sanders himself has given the following brief outline of the suffrage restrictions in his State, at the time when the " grandfather " clause was in force—for the registration of voters under it was concluded in 1898.

" There are in our suffrage law," explained Mr. Sanders, " three ways of securing registration as a voter.  In the first place, it was provided that if prior to September, 1898, a man could prove that either his father or his grandfather was entitled to vote in 1868 under the old constitution, he could be

at once registered.*  If he did not take advantage
of the grandfather clause before that time, he would
have to submit to the ordinary educational or property qualifications.  The lists made up in 1898 have
not been altered since then, and of course they concern only the people who were registered at that
time.

" Secondly, a man is permitted to register provided he can fill out the blank spaces in an ordinary
declaration which is printed in the constitution.  No
discretion is given to the election officers, and there
is no trickery at all.  The mere filling out of the
certificate which declares that the man believes himself a legal voter, that he was born at such and such
a place, at such and such a time, and that he is

* Louisiana Constitution, 1898:

ARTICLE 197.  *Section 5* (Suffrage and Elections).—No male
person who was on January 1, 1867, or at any date prior
thereto, entitled to vote under the Constitution, or statutes
of any State of the United States, wherein he then resided,
and no son or grandson of any such person not less than
twenty-one years of age at the date of the adoption of this
Constitution, and no male person of foreign birth, who was
naturalized prior to the first day of January, 1898, shall be
denied the right to register and vote in this State by reason
of his failure to possess educational or property qualifications
prescribed by this Constitution, provided, he shall have resided in this State for five years next preceding the date at
which he shall apply for registration, and shall have registered in accordance with the terms of this Article prior to
September 1, 1898, and no person shall be entitled to register
under this Section after said date.

therefore so many years, months, and days old, is complete evidence that he can read, write, and figure, and that he therefore has satisfied the requirements of the law.

"I myself opposed the proposition to introduce any trickery by requiring the applicant for registration to show that he understands the law. We require an ordinary test of ability to read and write English, and nothing but that. You will see, then, that under the Louisiana law a man may become a voter in any one of three different ways. If his name is on the list established in 1898 he can vote now; or if he can fill out the required certificate; or if he can show that he pays taxes on property of an assessed value of $300.

"So far as the law goes, there is absolutely no discrimination against the negro. There were free negroes in slavery days who had full political rights, and their descendants could have been put on the grandfather list in 1898. It so happens that I was put on that list, as a matter of precaution, and as I can read and write and pay some taxes I can claim the right to vote under either one of these three provisions of the law. Every other man, black or white, has the same right."

Speaking with the utmost frankness and with that honesty of purpose and directness of logic which have put him at the head of his profession in Louisiana, Mr. Sanders continued:

" We are willing to give to the negro every possible right except social and political equality. That we will prevent his having. We will prevent it as peaceably as we can, but you can be sure that we will prevent it. The Anglo-Saxon never brooks opposition from an inferior race, and white men will maintain their domination in Illinois as well as in Louisiana. This is a life-and-death matter with us, and every man who has actually lived among negroes understands this. I am quite well aware that this policy may have a bad effect politically outside the black belt, but it will be maintained, and it *must* be maintained, notwithstanding.

" Congress may cut down our representation, it may deprive us of both senators; but none the less we shall have to keep our control of affairs in our own community. Few of our negroes have voted since 1898. In the sugar parishes they are all labourers and in the cotton belt they are generally tenants. In either case, the white man owns the land and the negro is dependent on that for support, so that when he finds that we do not want him to vote, and insist on being allowed to run the politics of the community, he stays away from the polls. But he is not disfranchised by law in Louisiana, and that fact should be known to all people."

Reduced to the last analysis, all the laws that can be devised are futile finally to prevent the negro from exercising the right of suffrage. He is becoming educated, is acquiring property, and cannot be barred from the ballot by operation of law. But outside the law, the white man, after all, controls the situation. He is the employer of labour; commercially as well as industrially he is master of the situation. The " grandfather " clause, the " understanding " clause, and similar devices of politicians could readily be upset in the courts. But the white men are always able to insist that they will employ no negroes who go near the ballot box; that no black voters shall be accepted as tenants; and that coloured politicians shall not be sold the actual necessities of life.

In this way the white men have been enabled absolutely to destroy the coloured vote in the South; and the prospect seems to be that they will maintain the dominance of the Anglo-Saxon over the negro until the black man is so far raised in the social scale that he can be trusted, and that he shall cease to be a positive menace to the welfare of the community.

## IV

## Varying Views on the Suffrage Question

TWO of the foremost negro educators of the South, Booker T. Washington and Professor DuBois of Atlanta, represent radically differing points of view among the negroes themselves as regards their political status. The latter believes that the suffrage is necessary to the salvation of his people. In discussing the future of the negro and his manifest adaptability to the work of an artisan, Professor DuBois threw a curious light upon the influence of politics in the matter of industrial development and the earning of one's daily bread.

" Our negroes," he said, " have gone into almost every conceivable branch of trade here in Atlanta; they have quite generally joined the trade unions, but wherever there is a lack of work this is a distinct disadvantage to them. That is to say, when he does not belong to a trade union, the negro can frequently secure work which he needs by charging less for his labour than the white man. The white employer of labour will choose the cheaper labour, whether it be white or black. When the negro, however, is bound by union rules, and cannot cut under the card rates, he is immediately put at a disadvantage as compared with the white member of the same union. The employer will, if there is any discretion, give the job to the white labourer, because he has a vote, has a voice in the community, and is a factor to be reckoned with; whereas the coloured man, although a member of the same union, has neither social nor political influence. Thus it happens that when there is a lack of work it is the negro who is first out of a job, and who is not protected by his membership in the union, merely because of his lack of political influence in the community."

Mr. Washington, on the other hand, claims that it is not true that his people are either interested in politics or seeking office. When asked if he thought the time had come for the negro to insist on his right of suffrage in the South, he replied cautiously:

"It is well known that I take the position that no race in the economic and educational condition of the masses of the black people at the present time should make the matter of politics a question of first importance in connection with their development. There are other considerations which must precede and underlie political prominence. I make this statement not in speaking of the negro only, but as applicable to any people in the same stage of development.  I do believe, however, as I have often stated before in the South as in the North, that the negro should have constantly held out before him a hope of reward for right living; and the law that rewards righteous living should be the same for both races."

This latter sentence, of course, refers to the crying disgrace of the South, the one thing which must ultimately break down the present suffrage system by the force of honest public opinion, which is, that the educational tests generally adopted in the South apply to the negro only, while the ignorant and illiterate white man is everywhere permitted to vote.

The ideas of Booker Washington are heartily endorsed in the South, according to Clark Howell, editor of the *Atlanta Constitution*.  "The people of the South generally," he declares, "are in hearty accord with Booker Washington, and his effort for the settlement of the negro question.  They believe he has struck the keynote, and the Southern people will give him a hearty support in his efforts to keep the negroes out of politics and build up the industrial education of his race.

"Booker Washington's lesson is what the people of the North need most to learn.  Not only here but there, the negro who has mixed in politics in any way will insist that the salvation of the race can be achieved only through the ballot box.  These

men, and there are some of them right here in
Atlanta, are antagonizing Booker Washington instead of supporting him, and it is this antagonism
which is encouraged, in fact endorsed, by the appointment of negroes to important political positions in the Southern States."

Mr. Howell is enthusiastic in regard to the possibility of a settlement of the negro question, if the
people of the North, who are not immediately concerned, will only trust the people of the South to
settle the matter in the only way in which it can
possibly be adjusted.    Indeed, he even says " there
is no race question."

" Just let us alone," he said, " that is the whole
story.    Let us alone to settle this matter ourselves,
without interference, and the best interests of blacks
and whites will be taken care of.    By letting us
alone, I mean, for instance, that there should be no
appointment of negroes to important federal positions in high communities.    There is no possible
objection to the coloured man's going into subordinate positions in the civil service, like that of a let-
ter-carrier.    He is fitted for that kind of work, but
he is not fitted for the important places to which
he is appointed by the Republican presidents.    Remove the fear of negro domination and the Southern States will at once split up on ordinary economic
lines.    Several of them will surely go Republican.
When the people of the North understand this sit-

uation, the so-called negro question will be disposed of, and not before.

" The people of Georgia have at no time been afraid of an intelligent negro vote. It is the rule of the vicious and ignorant we fear. The best thought of the South, the men who are in the forefront of its modern progress, know it is not best to have only one party. Feeling, however, that the negro question is the paramount issue, we settle all of our political fights in the white primary, so that the actual vote cast at an election is but a fraction of that put into the ballot of the primary. The result is that the white voters of Georgia form a single political party. The negroes know this, and thus they make no attempt to vote. We have not found it necessary to resort to extraordinary educational qualifications."

Mr. Howell's summing up of his opinions on the subject was at once significant and sensible. " If the people of the North," he said, " devoted themselves as anxiously to getting work for the negro as they do to getting him the ballot, they would solve the negro question at once."

# THE SOLUTION

# I

## What the Negro Has Done for the Negro

ONE of the most advanced negro philanthropists in the country is Professor W. H. H. Hart. Born a slave in a stockade in Alabama, he had his first schooling from a Yankee " school-marm " under the shade of a forest on the banks of the Chattahoochee. By the road of the study of law he has progressed to membership of the bar in every court in the District of Columbia, and to the professorship of law in Howard University, of which he is a graduate. He has been assistant to the district attorney in his city, and assistant librarian of Congress. But besides all these achievements, he is head of a voluntary charitable institution of his own, known as the Hart Farm School, which since 1897 he has supported out of his own pocket.

Professor Hart knows the South as well, perhaps, as any man in the country, so far as racial characteristics are concerned; and as his own father and both his grandfathers were white men, he is perhaps as well equipped by training as any one can be to understand the tremendous issues involved in what is known as the negro question in the United States.

" No nostrums.  No miracles."  This is the text from which Professor Hart preaches a remarkable sermon.  It must be understood, in the first place, that he is broad enough and fair enough to talk conservatively, patiently, hopefully, and philosophically regarding a great question which he himself says will require generations to settle.  He takes the ground, fortifying his position with an astonishing grasp of the actual situation in the United States, that the negro is nothing more nor less than a man, not peculiar in any sense, but to be dealt with as other men would be dealt with, when placed in exactly the same circumstances.

Granting at once that ignorance is the great bar to progress, Professor Hart insists that education through the medium of the common school is the only solution of the race problem in America.  Furthermore, he insists that the South is not entirely to blame for the illiteracy of the blacks, and that it is the duty of the nation at large to provide a national school fund adequate to eliminate the ignorant negro from the problem altogether.  The South, he says, is too poor to do this work itself; and as the illiterate negroes, ignorant from no fault of their own, are none the less a menace to the safety of the whole republic, it therefore becomes the duty of the nation at large, by the use of the national funds, to stamp out illiteracy in the South just as it would stamp out an epidemic of yellow fever in human beings, or of the " foot and mouth disease " in cattle.

This remarkable man is a quadroon; in his veins there runs but one-fourth part of negro blood. All the rest is white; but under the old and the present laws he is none the less a negro. If he were not so by law he would be by inclination, for he has devoted his life to an entirely practical and successful effort to better certain portions of his own race, dividing his time and energy between his instruction at Howard University, where coloured men and women are given a remarkably good higher education, and his personal charitable work. The Farm School began upon a farm which its founder owned a few miles down the Potomac from Washington, where years ago Professor Hart set out to create a home for the little coloured waifs of the capital. About 1900 Congress recognized it as a successful charity, and passed a small appropriation in its aid. But until that time and since then, every cent accruing from a successful law practice was devoted to the work, which is in the nature of a voluntary reform school. The little street criminals were actually put on their honour, and with entire success. No bolts, no bars, no guards, no high walls labelled this novel institution as a reformatory. Each little coloured chap was told that his own interest was involved in remaining at the school; and to the everlasting credit of the " little cusses " be it said that few of them ever have run away, and most of those who have, came back of their own accord.

This single paragraph can in no way be a fair treatment of so extensive a work as that of Professor Hart. But the reference to that work shows the kind of man he is, and accentuates the value of his observations upon the race question. He has studied the possibilities, the racial tendencies, and especially the criminology of the negro in a place where he comes in the most favourable circumstances into contact with the whites. And he has spent all his own money on the work of uplifting the class of negroes from which criminals are made, never soliciting a dollar from outside sources. The money voted by Congress is sufficient only for a small part of the running expenses, and all the land, all the buildings, the cost of supervision, and the building up of permanent improvements, have been contributed alone and unaided by this devoted negro philanthropist. His work gives a suggestion of the way in which the negro problem is to be solved; apparently the responsibility of the individual plays a large part in Professor Hart's idea of the solution.

Atlanta, that splendid new metropolis of the new

South, is the seat of a number of the most important educational institutions for the coloured people. From the time of Sherman's famous capture of this city, Northern philanthropists began the work of education from this centre. The negro forms only one-third of the population, and is not much in evidence on the streets; but he fills fully one-half of the places in the industrial world, and so is closely associated with the city and feels a pride in it. Quite the most interesting feature of the negro life here is Atlanta University, and one of the most cultivated of negro men is Professor W. E. Burghardt DuBois of the chair of economics and history in that institution.

To reach the room of Dr. DuBois, one trudges up two flights of stairs, through bare, uncarpeted college halls, and at the top finds himself suddenly transported into the busy literary workshop of a close student. Seated at the centre of a big table, revolving easily in his office chair, alert, intelligent, conservative, weighing his words cautiously, and yet speaking with the confidence born of profound study, the picture of this brown-skinned, well-dressed, self-poised scholar was one not soon to be forgotten. Eliminate the question of colour, which of course is a mere matter of taste, and the picture would be that of an exceedingly attractive man. He has accomplished a European cut to his short whisker which tells of training abroad; and while

he possesses all the easy bearing of the cultured
gentleman, there is not the slightest trace of the
forwardness and presumption which Southern white
men invariably ascribe to the negro of mixed blood,
no matter what his position.

Dr. DuBois is an excellent specimen in proof of
the possibilities of the New England training. In
his person he gives the lie to the frequently circulated statements that the negro is not susceptible of
real culture. Born in the Massachusetts town of
Great Barrington, in the heart of the Berkshires,
he had excellent opportunity to show what can be
done for the negro in the way of education when
he is thrown among the right surroundings. He
played with the little Yankee boys, unconsciously
assimilated to himself their condition of culture, received an excellent education, went to Harvard,
studied in the Fisk University at Nashville, and
completed his education abroad among the scholars
of Germany, where he was treated as an equal, lived
in a German family, and had all the advantages of
German culture.

With such a training, it is difficult to understand
at first how such a man could have betaken himself
to the backwoods and taught a little country school
for coloured children, until one realizes that even in
the North, a cultivated negro gentleman can be completely isolated by the operation of the rules of
caste. He could turn with positive enthusiasm to

a life like that at the Atlanta University, where the white people of the city do not receive him in any capacity, but where he finds a cultivated set of people, who, like himself, are devoted to the uplifting of the negro and to the solving of the great race question, which seems now to be the most puzzling and the most profound in American social life.

Dr. DuBois is not only interesting as an object lesson of the value of education and environment for the negro, but he also has the peculiar racial characteristics.  He is a mulatto and the child of mulattoes, who were also the children of mulattoes, the white strain being three and four generations back. Mrs. DuBois, it is interesting to note, is the daughter of a mulatto and a white German woman. Who could be better qualified to speak of his race, its instincts, its possibilities, and its aspirations, than this Northern-born, Harvard-bred, mixed-blooded negro, about as much white as black, who voluntarily subjects himself to complete social ostracism in the South, to labour for the future advancement of his own people?

" Somehow there never was a place for me," said Dr. DuBois in discussing his early life in the North. " During my earliest boyhood days, I knew no difference between me and the other boys about me. They treated me as an equal, and I did not realize in any way what it meant to be coloured.  My first

intimation was that during the summer vacations,
as I grew older, the other boys were able to earn
a little money as clerks in stores or in similar positions, but there never was a vacancy for me in
those Yankee stores.  People were glad to have
me mow their lawns, water their grass, and do
similar odd jobs, but I never could get the same
opportunity the white boy had, even though this
was New England.  I remember only too well little
uneducated, almost outcast Irish boys, who lived
on the street with me and with whom I would not
think of associating.  They had their opportunities,
however; could find their way into stores where
there was a chance to rise; and they all did rise,
in business, in politics, and in social life, while I
was stranded in my manhood just where I was in
my boyhood.

"The Northern people think they have opened
the door of hope, but they have never stopped to
think that it does not lead anywhere.  They have
given the negro the franchise and he is treated as
an equal before the law, and for that all credit is
due the North.  But the negro has no opportunity
in business; he cannot secure a subordinate place
in a business house with the slightest prospect of
promotion, no matter how faithful, how intelligent,
how determined to succeed he may be.  There is a
constant lack of opportunity for the coloured youth,
and if he becomes idle, if he becomes careless and

indifferent to the interests of his employers, it is because he has become doomed to remain in a subordinate capacity, and he knows it. Even in the liberty-loving North there is for him no chance of promotion, no incentive for good work. The negro in the North is not sufficiently numerous yet to have a cultivated society of his own, except in a few large centres. He is, therefore, isolated, and while the Northern people believe they treat him with utmost fairness, the messenger boy in the store never becomes a salesman, the carpenter never becomes a foreman, and the hotel bell-boy is never put behind the desk."

This gentle indictment of the effect of caste in that North which is seeking impudently to settle the negro question for the South was delivered without the slightest trace of passion. A story which Dr. DuBois told me of his experiences in Germany was also suggestive of his attitude. He and a young German, who looked like a Jew but was not, were calling upon some German girls. The young women manifested some signs of displeasure, which young DuBois thought was directed at him. His companion instantly explained, however. "They think I am a Jew, and therefore they resent associating with me. You are not concerned. This is a race question, and you do not understand such prejudices."

"As if I didn't understand race prejudices only

too well, and a thousand times better than he did,"
commented the narrator.

In explaining his work at Atlanta, he continued:
" Teachers are absolutely necessary to the education
of the negro masses. Hence schools and colleges
for the higher education of the negro must be supported and maintained in the South before you can
possibly hope to wipe out illiteracy among the
masses. About one million out of three millions
of negro children are actually going to school. The
need for teachers is so great that the field cannot be
filled for many years to come, no matter how hard
we work. Thus it is true that institutions for the
higher education of the negro have an abundant
field, if it were nothing more than to supply teachers, because it is quite manifest that you cannot
secure teachers for common schools except by giving them a higher education than the common
schools afford. Such statistics as we have been enabled to get show that about fifty per cent of the
graduates of negro colleges become teachers, and
it goes without saying that they are teachers of
their own race.

" In one of the recent social studies conducted by
the university, it was figured out that of the negro
college graduates over half are teachers, one-sixth
are preachers, another sixth are students and professional men, over six per cent are farmers,
artisans, and merchants, and four per cent are in

the government service. Our negro physicians are succeeding much better from a financial standpoint than any other class of professional men. They are practising, of course, almost exclusively among coloured people, but in Atlanta, in Washington, in Philadelphia, in Chicago, and in other large centres there are negro physicians who are making fine incomes, and you must remember one on Pennsylvania Avenue in Washington who runs his own automobile on his daily rounds.

"Most of our college graduates who leave us in June find something to do by September. It is not at all true, as they say here, that the highly educated negro in the South finds no field of occupation and goes North. On the contrary, he is working here among his own race, and is almost invariably successful."

If Dr. DuBois is able to argue convincingly for the higher education of the negro, the other side is not unsupported, even by the negro himself. Every one knows Tuskegee. Every one knows Booker T. Washington, the man among a million who has conceived and executed the greatest work now being done for his race. It is not necessary to go into detail as to the life history or personal characteristics of the great leader. The most striking traits in his personality are his modest self-confidence, the directness and intentness of his intellectual methods, and the extreme simplicity and

honesty of his daily life.  He could not be less
ostentatious if he were at the head of a little barber
shop, instead of being the principal of a great institution with a cash capital of over a million, with
tweny-five hundred acres of land, with seventeen
hundred students, and with a special endowment
providing for the life-time needs of the principal
himself.

Talking over the general plans of this institution, which, as every one knows, is built up on the
theory of teaching the negro how to use his hands
intelligently in useful trades, in agriculture, and
in the foundation of industrial life, I called attention to the fact that it was being asserted that the
educated negro found nothing to do after he came
out of school and college, and was forced either
to go North or to slip back into the social condition from which he emerged when he went to
school.

" It is not at all true within our experience," said
the principal, leaning back in his office chair, with
his hands in the pockets of a commodious seer-
sucker coat, " that the educated negro fails to find
work in the South and is driven northward.  On
the contrary, the literary colleges find it difficult to
supply the demand for teachers; and I am quite
positive, so far as our own students go, that those
who are trained in the industrial pursuits can find
instant employment.  In fact, the great difficulty

is to keep them here during an entire course, because they find opportunities of employment at comparatively high prices long before they are ready for graduation, and the temptation to go out into the world for themselves is frequently more than they can withstand. The development of the South along industrial lines has become so great that the demand for artisans in all classes of trades is far in excess of the supply.

" The favourite trades of the students here seem to be bricklaying, carpentering, and tailoring.    I presume they apply for instruction in these trades because the demand is greatest outside in those particular lines.    There is, however, practically an equal demand for millwrights, plumbers, wagonmakers, and gas-fitters; and we have a great many letters asking for graduates to take charge of dairy farms.    Our needs here in Tuskegee have led us to pay more than ordinary attention to the building trades.    We have had to get housed, and the problem has been by no means a small one.    Counting students, teachers, and children in the families, we have to provide for about seventeen hundred people at a time, and this has kept us busy with new buildings, all of which have been put up, designed, decorated, and in most cases furnished complete by our own negro labour."

Asked if he saw at Tuskegee any indication of the truth of the charge so frequently made by the white man, that the negro has a deficient intellectual capacity and cannot succeed in any occupation which requires the use of the reasoning faculties to any great extent, Dr. Washington replied that he had never yet discovered any indication of any bar to the intellectual growth of the negro. " His reasoning power," he said, " seems to be as well developed as any other mental trait. Allowing for early associations, and for the negro's lack of home training, his logical capacity seems to be about the same as that of the whites. In fact, the race is developing along lines which have necessitated the use of its reasoning faculties to an extraordinary degree, and under conditions in which there could not have been success without these reasoning faculties.

" For instance, we used to have great difficulty in securing negroes to handle our electric plant, and of course to give instructions in that department as well, for everything here must be viewed from the educational standpoint. We also found it hard to discover men properly trained in mechanical and agricultural drawing, or to conduct chemical experiments for the agricultural department, or who were educated in general scientific work. Now all this has been changed. The scientific departments can readily be equipped with negroes who have a highly technical training. This indicates pretty clearly that the capacity of the coloured man is not at fault, because he is beginning to demonstrate his ability along lines which absolutely require the accurate use of the reasoning faculties.

" It is true, however, that the negro is lacking in foresight. He does not, as a class, look ahead, and he is frequently quite improvident with both time and money, but that is not a constitutional fault.

" Our own students here are being trained in scientific agriculture, and we are seeking to teach them the reasons for things, so that they may act intelligently. The graduates of our agricultural department have been almost uniformly successful as individual farmers."

Frequently in the South the charge is made that the education given to negro women at Tuskegee unfits them for domestic service instead of training them for it, giving them exalted ideas and ambitions which render them unfitted for real life, and which result in the long run in mental, if not moral degradation. I asked, accordingly, whether the school was essentially designed to teach the women domestic service, and so arranged as not to give them false ideas.

" We do train our students here," said this conservative observer, who discussed the talents and feelings of his own race so dispassionately, " in the highest grades of domestic service. No girl who graduates here at Tuskegee can possibly feel above going into domestic service, because we especially and above all teach them the dignity of labour in all directions.    That is the foundation stone of this school.    It is quite true, nevertheless, that you will not find many of our women graduates actually engaged in household work, either here or in the North.    The reason for this is that the girls who graduate here have received a training which enables them to command wages of from five to ten dollars a week and even higher.    This is much more than they can hope to earn in any ordinary household work, at least here in the South, where the average rate of pay for this kind of employment is from eight to ten dollars a month."

## II

## The Southerner's Point of View

A N interesting statement of the negro problem
and its outcome, from the viewpoint of the
average Southerner of education, is outlined
in the following discussion of the matter by one of
the most intellectual and broad-minded men in the
quaint old city of Savannah. His point of view is
not as cold-blooded nor as relentless as it seems, for
it must be admitted that the policy of white domination is a matter of actual self-preservation for the
Southern States, where in many a county equal political rights could only result in submerging the intelligent portion of the community beneath a
strangling wave of semi-barbarity. There was a
certain placid philosophy in this man's elabora-
tion of his theory of the relation between the
races.

" This is a white man's country," was his starting
point. " The white men earned their own civilization, and cut their own way to the place they now
occupy. They do not propose to share that place
with a race of men which is at best centuries behind
the white people in development.

" We will take care of the negro, we will educate him, we will look after him; but he must be subordinated for all time to come to the stronger race. He may be a political equal some day, but he cannot be now. We will not receive him in our homes on terms of equality; we will not associate with him in business enterprises; and we will not give him political equality if we can help it. But we will be faithful as the white man always is faithful toward a down-trodden and manifestly inferior race.

" There is no race question in America. The white men are bound to run things, whether in Illinois or in Georgia, and the negro will survive where the Indian perished merely because he does not resist. If he did resist he would be annihilated. This condition is not peculiar to the South, for the Indian was driven out of New England quite as relentlessly as out of Georgia, and if over fifty per cent of the population of Chicago were black to-day, as they are in Savannah, the white men of Chicago would keep control just the same as they do here in the schools, in the courts, in the churches, and in the homes.

" The black man must be subordinated for many generations to come; and even when he reaches a plane of comparative equality he must still remain a separate factor in the community; he cannot become amalgamated, except perhaps at the expiration of hundreds of years.

" The white people have made themselves the masters of the world—not by conciliation, and not always by merit, but because when they found a race of men unwilling or unfit to amalgamate with them, they promptly pushed their enemies out of the way. It must be so always. Here in Georgia we fought the Indian with all the power at our command until as late as 1840. There are no Indians in Georgia now, because the Indian resisted the encroachment of the whites and was swept out of the way. The salvation of the negro lies in the fact that he is of a weak race. He does not fight. He never resists in a body. Now and then he kills a single white man, but it is through fear and not through resentment. The result is that the negro will survive where the red man perished, although the negro is infinitely less desirable as a citizen, and although the Indian has been successfully bred into the white race without any feeling of disgust being created by the union.

" We people here in the South do not like to discuss the negro question, because we do not like to attack the race as a whole. They were brought up with us in our childhood, and we all know many clean, honest, loyal, and moral coloured people. Their number is even growing as the result of education and civilization. It is a painful fact, however, of which we do not talk, merely to save the feelings of the better class of negroes, that the great mass of their race is deep in a barbaric immorality, of the extent of which the Northern people have no conception.

"You must bear in mind the fact that the negro, as we have him here to-day, is at the best not over a century away from the grossest and most debasing savagery. The morals of the savage, including the negro quite as much as the Indian, are little better than those of the animal; and this embraces both sexes. Part of this is due to the debasing effect of slavery, but a greater part of it is hereditary instinct, traceable over the one short century to a life of absolute degradation, no better than that of the wild beasts with which the African negro was surrounded.

"It would be difficult to find a community of white men where there were many openly living in idleness upon the fruits of the sale of their wives, their mothers, and their sisters. These are harsh words, I know, but the people of the North must face the truth. The black man as he exists in the South to-day is unfit for any association with white men or white women. As he becomes educated he will grow out of all this, but until he does grow out of it it is manifest that he must be treated as an inferior.

"This question of the immorality of the blacks is one seldom referred to by Southern men, but their silence is a matter of abstract kindness towards these poor barbarians. The existence of this gross immorality, which perhaps could better be called unmorality, is not even a matter of argument. It can be and will be eradicated by the schools and the churches, but at the present time it still exists in an appalling degree.

" Amalgamation has practically stopped here in the South. Every time I go North I am told—especially in New York—of cases where black men have married white women. I do not know how common these marriages are, but they are not important, because the number of coloured people in the North is comparatively so small. Here in the South it is quite evident that the mulatto is dying out, not at all because he is of poor constitution, but because the supply has stopped. The half-breed is not marrying among the whites but among the blacks, and the result is a shading off of the negroes from pure black to brown, and the gradual elimination of the quadroon and the octoroon.

" Improper relations between the white men and black women are extremely rare nowadays. Such relations at one time were at least not unusual, but to-day a white man even of the lowest class who should openly admit that he sustained improper relations with a woman of the black race would be shunned by every one, and probably would be driven out of his community, if not by force at least by the impulse of public opinion. The mulatto children are becoming fewer and fewer, and they are the result almost entirely of unions between negro women and the lower class of white men who have come here from the North and have not been here long enough to understand that such unions are revolting to the mass of the community here.

" If the Republicans had not made such an awful blunder from a political standpoint by attempting to give the negro the ballot, the white race ultimately would have been at the mercy of the blacks in the South. This seems paradoxical, but it is true. If the Northern people had freed the negro and then let him alone entirely, the result would have been that the Southern whites would have been forced to do a great deal for the negro from mere sympathy. They would have found him even more beggared than they were themselves, and they would have taken him up, helped him along, and provided for him as they did during slavery days, at the same time allowing him to remain a free agent.

" The black man was faithful to us all during the war. He preserved our buried silverware, he took faithful care of our wives and children, he did not betray his trust at any time, although he well understood that the success of the Yankee army meant his freedom. The relations between the master and the man were such after the war that if left alone, the loyalty of the black man to the white would have been as strong as ever. As a result, when in the fulness of time they were given the ballot, the blacks would all have been Democrats like their masters. We should thus have built up on terms of comparative equality an alien black race, united to us by political ties, fostered by a friendly supervision, and made so strong that in the end they must have controlled the destinies of the South.

" But the attempt to give the negro the ballot, his appointment to important offices, and the horrible events of the reconstruction period, opened the eyes of all in the South to the danger which threatened them. They saw that they could not afford to foster the idea of equality between white and black, either at the polls or anywhere else. So the sympathy between the old slave-holding class and their former slaves was wiped out by the attempt to give the negro the ballot.

" The failure of that attempt was the best thing that ever happened to the South. It forced us to learn what I said at first, that this is a white man's government, and that the republic itself cannot possibly exist except under the government of white men. The negroes themselves recognize this fact now, and the more intelligent of them readily admit that their attempt to secure equal rights by means of the ballot was worse than failure, because they have now not only been deprived of the ballot under colour of law, but they have also seen fade away from them the old sympathy, the pity, and paternal protection which the white people of the South extended to the negro before the war, and which the negro to this day cannot do without.

"Just leave the negroes alone. Remember that we are dealing with a problem as old as the world. Modern civilization, such as we know it, dates from Cromwell and from Luther. It was born of civil and religious liberty. It has taken us a long time to get where we are now, and yet we have behind us traditions and hereditary influences all the way from Moses, Phidias, and St. Paul.

"The negro is a century out of savagery. Give him time, and he will build himself up far above the plane upon which he now is; but in the nature of things he can hardly hope to catch up with the white man, who will be progressing at the same time.

"The field of the American negro, I firmly believe, is in Africa. That great dark continent is as yet almost wholly uncivilized. The British, the Germans, and the French are shooting bullets into the black people over there, but they are not building schoolhouses nor starting newspapers, and they have not even begun to teach the African negro how to help himself, as we have taught the American negro.

"The battle for civilization which must be waged in Africa can best be led by the American negro. He is the natural missionary to his own race, and he could profitably go back there, not as an individual, but in communities. We should send back to Africa not our own ignorant and degraded negroes, but our best, our most moral, and our most highly educated negroes. As fast as we complete in them the work of civilization, they can be absorbed readily in the missionary work of Africa. As to their position in this country, no man who has studied the question at first hand can possibly expect to see the negro anything but an inferior. He is not a white man with a black skin, and he will always be centuries behind the white man in the race for a still higher and better civilization.

" In spite of the fact that the negroes pay only three per cent of the entire school tax of the South, we are now turning out about 100,000 educated negroes annually. Of these, about 10,000 find places here in the South. The remaining 90,000 find it impossible to secure positions which are in accord with all their new dignity as educated men. They have the idea quite generally that education is more or less a white man's trick, by means of which he manages to live without working. The educated negro will not work in the field, nor do hard manual labour. Our educated surplus of 90,000, therefore, is all going North. The Northern States are getting every year about as many negroes as there are now in the State of Illinois.

" We could not afford to have the movement of

population progress too rapidly, or we should be out of labourers. As a matter of fact, however, there is a counter current. Year by year, farmers from the North and the Northwest are selling out farms worth one hundred dollars an acre, coming South, and buying equally as good land at from three to ten dollars an acre. These men are taking the place of the negro; and in my judgment the time is not far distant when the agriculture of the South, except perhaps the cotton, will be in the hands of these Northern farmers, who are bringing with them energy, new methods, a little surplus capital, and the willingness to work with their hands; and who reach the conviction almost immediately after their arrival that the negro is desirable neither as an employee nor as a neighbour.

"So it is that our surplus of educated negroes, most of them, is going northward, and the Northern farmers are coming southward, an operation by which every one must at once see that the South is the gainer."

# III

## Theories of Solution

IN the case of the negro problem, as in almost every other problem whose solution has not yet been worked out by experience, there are almost as many theories suggested as to how to solve it as there are individuals interested in the subject. No theory can be established till it has stood the test of time and of actual experiment; yet some seem more practicable than others. Among the Southerners who cling to the old ideal of emigration as the best means of disposing of the negro is a certain well-known citizen of Charleston, whose view differs, however, from that of most educated Southern whites. He argues as follows, with Stanley's " Darkest Africa " as a basis for his argument:

" Our negroes were from the Congo country. When they were captured by the slave traders they were already slaves to black men, and their ancestors had been before them for centuries. They were the lowest and most degraded of the African negroes.

" There was a wave of African emigration from Persia down the east coast of the continent which represented the best element in Africa. This is only a fringe, however, and can be traced to this day, including tribes like the Zulus and similar African races, whose people are fighters.

" I remember when I was a boy on the plantation there were certain men among the slaves who were constantly being punished by the overseers, who fought against slavery, who ran away to the swamps, and who rebelled against the white man in every possible direction. These men generally had much better minds than the others, and were possessed of native ferocity, both of which qualities can be accounted for by the fact that they were straggling members of the superior nations of Africa, who had been swept along with the great wave of Congo slaves.

" Our black man, brought to us by the slave traders and paid for with New England guns and glass beads, was a degraded creature. I say this not to attack the negroes at all, but simply to explain what the people of the South have long understood and what the people of the North seem determined not to understand, that we have to deal with a creature so low in the scale of human intelligence at the start that he is necessarily unfitted for association with the whites. It will take generations of training here to obliterate the degradation of generations of slavery in Africa before he came here."

The remedy which this student of the race problem unhesitatingly proposed was the return of the negroes to Africa.  " This," he said, " must be done by government action.  I would not attempt to ship all the negroes at once, nor would I do it by force or indiscriminately.  I would train the negro as well as I could here, and endeavour to make things so pleasant for him in Liberia that it would be a prize to secure transportation to his native land.

" Clement Irons, a negro, made a successful start in this direction and took a black colony to Liberia, which I believe is eminently successful.  The negro is the natural missionary to uplift Africa, and I cannot understand why our people in the South have opposed the emigration of the negro and have adopted restrictive laws, such as that which drove out of the country the famous ' Peg Leg Williams,' who was seeking to secure labour for the North.

" If the coloured people are encouraged to secure their political rights in the South at the present time, there will be bloodshed in the long run.  The horrors of reconstruction no man can tell.  They cannot be repeated.  This is a white man's country, and you cannot logically insist that the negro shall exercise political functions so long as you bar out the Chinaman and refuse to allow him to become naturalized.  The North was wise enough to see its danger in this respect before it was too late. If we ever let down the bars now raised against the

Chinese, the North will have a race question of its
own, which it would solve exactly as we are solving ours here in the South, by holding the control
of the government at all hazards."

A less drastic and more practicable, if somewhat
easy-going method is that advocated by Mr. Stone
of Greenville, already quoted in these pages, who
believes in letting things take care of themselves,
leaving time to work out the solution, by natural
processes.   Nothing can be done, as he thinks, to
render race friction less acute, except to wait.  " No
ill-tempered agitation," said he, " either by whites
or by negroes, will do the slightest good.   I believe,
however, that the people of the North are gradually coming to understand that the South is confronted with a great social problem, and that the
South must solve it sooner or later.   If the negro
could be dispersed throughout the entire country
it is true that he would be swallowed up, but this
is an impossibility at the present time.   The negro
has no money to move away, and besides that, his
labour is necessary to the continued prosperity of
the South, unless we can find a substitute for it.
Few Northern men understand either the peculiar
characteristics of the negro and his inability to take
care of himself, or the generally friendly attitude
of the Southern people towards him.   We do not
hate the negro; Northern people who say so are
simply ignorant of the situation.   We were brought

up with the negro, and I think we understand his capacity and are much more tender for his faults than Northern people would be. In return for this the South should have credit for an honest desire to do the best thing possible for the negro. We need his labour; it is to our interest to make him self-supporting, inasmuch as the South is an agricultural country, and inasmuch as there is no living being who knows so well how to take care of the cotton plant as the American negro."

Clark Howell, the Atlanta editor, believes that work is the solution of the vexed question. He believes that his city is solving the problem in the right way. "Just look out of that window there," he said one day in his office, pointing to a huge skyscraper in process of erection. I could readily see that a decided majority of the workmen engaged upon it was coloured. They were working apparently in entire harmony with their white associates, laying brick, setting iron beams, doing the ordinary constructive work, an integral part of the marvellous revolution going on here in the commercial and industrial metropolis of the South.

"Just look at those men," continued the editor. "They don't need any politics, because they have work, and they are doing work for which they are eminently fitted. Come down here on Labour Day and you can see the coloured members of the different unions marching in the same parade with white workmen.   The negro makes an excellent artisan, and by supplying him with work for which he is adapted we are doing the proper thing to solve the so-called negro question, which is not a race question so much as one of the adjustment of social differences."

Sitting later with Mr. Howell on the broad veranda of the Piedmont Driving Club, and looking up the beautiful valley through which Sherman marched after the decisive battle of Peach Tree Creek, I listened as the editor told of how as a boy he made his pocket money by gathering up the flattened bullets which he raked out of the ground of the old intrenchments.   And I began to wonder that the Southern white people, who suffered so much and so recently first by the war and then by reconstruction, are so temperate, so patient, and so conservative in the presence of a political and social question which seems to threaten their very existence.

There are undoubtedly two sides to the negro question, and it is probably quite true that the Southern whites are not altogether right in their methods.   It is also true, however, that they are on the ground, that they are the people most affected, and that those persons in the North who are too vigorously shouting for an immediate adjustment of this great problem ought to learn a lesson in temperateness and courtesy from these

young men of the new South, who are patiently
waiting until the North comes around to their opinion, and who, in the meantime, with unique bravery,
if perhaps through some mistaken notions, have
successfully turned backward a great black wave
which they believed was about to overwhelm
them.

Casual observation about the streets of Atlanta by
day and at night, with some walks and drives into
the country, tend to confirm the statement made by
Mr. Howell that when a sufficiency of the proper
kind of work is provided for the negro the race
question, as a question, disappears.

Atlanta is the focus of a great industrial and
commercial revolution, the like of which has not
often been seen, but which is nearly equal to the
marvellous growth of Chicago. The city has grown
beyond all belief; the country round about is prosperous; there is plenty of money for legitimate commercial operations; cotton is enormously high, and
the negro is sharing in the general prosperity.

Atlanta is something like twelve hundred feet
above the sea level, and there is something in the
air which produces energy and progressiveness.
The negroes have caught this spirit on the bound.
In Charleston and in Savannah, even on the busiest
down town streets, there are scores and hundreds
of idle, ragged, frequently dissolute negroes. I
was told by one negro that his people did not like

Atlanta overmuch, but preferred the old-fashioned Southern towns, like Charleston and Jacksonville, the latter being, he said, the paradise of the lazy Southern negro. But in Atlanta no excuse is made for an idle negro, and the lazy ones drift away to other places, where their presence on the streets is not a subject of comment, while one sees an extraordinarily small number of negroes on the streets of Atlanta. The negro population is at work as far as one can judge, and is correspondingly contented and peaceable. The condition of things is a proof of the good sense and value of the industrial answer to the negro question. There are some old-fashioned and decaying Southern cities which would be much better off financially and socially if they could find work for all the negroes who are willing to work, and drive all the others out of the city, as Atlanta has done.

An experiment of this industrial sort was once tried in Charleston, whose citizens believed that they had discovered what to do with the negro when they started a cotton mill, to be run with negro labour. Ex-Mayor Smyth told of the outcome. "At first," he said, "it seemed as if the mill were to be a great success. The negro is a good imitator, he readily learned the work of the cotton mill, and while he was at work proved himself a valuable man.

"The difficulty which we had not anticipated

arose from the fact that the negro would not under any circumstances work steadily. The minute he got a little money ahead he would quit entirely until the money was gone. This was fatal to the cotton mill experiment, because the successful manufacture of such a product requires the continued operation of the machinery by skilled labour. The cotton mill proved a failure for no other reason than this unwillingness of the negro to work steadily, so that we could depend upon the constant supply of workmen who would know how to operate the machinery. The machinery in the Charleston cotton mill was taken to pieces and set up again at Gainesville, where it was afterwards destroyed by a cyclone."

Dr. DuBois, the Atlanta educator, also inclines toward an industrial solution, but not so much along lines of providing work as of industrial education. According to him, the work of negro upbuilding is a much wider thing than in the accepted view of it. " We have to do," he said, " not only with the millions of coloured people here in the United States, but with the other millions in the islands and the rest of America, and ultimately with the hundreds of millions who still remain in degradation in Africa."

His plan of campaign would be a concentration of effort for higher education among half a dozen colleges in the Southern States. " The course of

instruction in the others should be curtailed so as
to give them the rank of academies and preparatory
schools, to correspond about with the New England high school grade.   Just now we have too
many institutions which are intermediate between
the high school and the smaller New England
college.  If we could have a half-dozen good institutions of the New England college type, better
than normal schools and not so ambitious as great
universities, supplemented with a dozen or twenty
first-class academies of the high school grade, we
would then be prepared to attack the problem of the
primary education of the negro, and to reach the
two-thirds of the negro population now outside of
school influence.   There is need not of one Tuskegee, but of a dozen.   Mr. Washington is not doing
more than to take care of the material in his own
State, and the example he has set should be followed
by the establishment of at least one similar institution in every State in the South."

That able lawyer and philanthropist of Washington, Mr. Hart, advocates the need of both education and the suffrage as the salvation for his people.
To the question, "What is the matter with the
South, and what must be done about it?" he replied,
with the following scholarly treatment of the
subject:

"The greatest blight upon the Southern States
is still the one influence of slavery, from which

neither blacks nor whites have been able to escape.
Yet the interests of both black and white in the
South are identical.  What helps one helps the
other, and a hindrance to one is a hindrance to the
other.  They are actually neighbours now, and they
ought to be friends.

" The South to-day has marvellous natural resources, scarcely yet touched, and a widely scattered
and sparse population.  Its marshes are undrained,
its streams unbridged, its richest land undeveloped.
It holds the monopoly of one of the essential products of civilization—cotton.  The Western States,
Russia, Argentina, and Australia will feed the
world, but the south Atlantic States, with their
fields of fleece, must clothe the world.  The demand
for cotton will increase but the area of production
cannot be enlarged.  With such a staple in its possession, what is known as the black belt of America
must necessarily be prosperous from a material
point of view, and white and black alike must be
the beneficiaries of that prosperity.

" To develope these extraordinary resources there
is need of two things and two things only.  First
of all, there must be capital, and that capital must
come from without the South.  Secondly, there must
be a development of citizenship, and this element
must come from within the South.  There is need
to have the people educated in the knowledge of the
possibilities of the country and in the skill of turn-

ing those possibilities to account. This can be done in no other way but in the schools.

"There is a crying need throughout the whole South for common-school facilities. There is nothing which approaches the common-school system of the North and Northwest. The ignorance is not entirely confined to the coloured people, but there are many rural whites in the South who have practically no education, not from any fault of their own but because the country is too poor to give it. The difference in communities is in the men, and the difference in the men is in their mental development. Harvard, Brown, Yale, Dartmouth, Williams, are the causes which have made and still make New England different from New Guinea."

In further analysis of the actual conditions in the South to-day, this quadroon philosopher continued: "The excessive conservatism of the South grows out of the passions and the prejudices of her past history. The only way to overcome this is to develope another passion which shall be stronger than the one it is to supplant. That, it seems to me, must be the passion of an enlightened self-interest, which desires for itself the same progress which has resulted in the prosperity and the happiness of other communities. There must be a willingness to take the same means which have been found effective in other places to accomplish this result.

" Just at the present time the South is showing a disposition towards self-examination as to educational needs. This is the thin edge of the wedge. Sentiments, views, and policies from without are proving helpful in readjusting matters in the South in harmony with the inexorable demands of modern progress.

" The great pity of it all is that the South has not the means to provide school facilities which shall approach in completeness those in the East and the great West. The war did two terrible things to the South. It exhausted its resources and it destroyed its most promising manhood. Poverty retards progress, and poverty enforces and continues the illiteracy of the South. Senator Blair was the one statesman since Lincoln who proposed an adequate and certain means of relief which should put the South on an equal footing with the rest of the country. The failure of his educational bill and his retirement from Congress was a calamity to the South. The Southern people, the country, and the world will appreciate this fact more and more as time passes, and· will suffer more and more keenly, until public sentiment compels the enactment of just such a law as was proposed by Senator Blair.

" The country owes it to the South to aid her in every way to change the present conditions, which are crushing her industries and which threaten the peace and prosperity of the entire country.  There is no reason why a national educational fund cannot be provided and distributed in proportion to the illiteracy of the different States.  Our institutions demand the education of the masses, and the whole country must, in the nature of things, provide the common school for the great ignorant masses of the coloured population in the South.  It is unfair to expect the whites of the Southern States to bear the entire burden.  The negro question is both national and sectional, and the self-interest of the nation itself requires that an end shall be put once and for all to the terrible illiteracy among the negroes of the South.

" So much for education.  Now as to the question of suffrage for the negro.  The writ of the Declaration of Independence must run throughout the land.  A house divided against itself cannot stand.  The nation cannot endure half free and half unfree, nor one-third unfree, nor one-tenth unfree.  This is the foundation principal of our institutions as declared by Jefferson, Madison, Adams, Lincoln, Wendell Phillips, Whittier, and Charles Sumner.  The door of hope, the field of opportunity must be open, must be unobstructed for all men under the flag.  That is the inevitable end to which the whole people must come, and it is toward this end that we must begin the uplifting and upbuilding of the ten millions of coloured people under the stars and stripes.

" There must be no nostrums and there can be no
miracles.   The negro is no better and no worse
than any other man under similar conditions, similar environment, and similar heredity.

" The negro is no angel either of light or of dark-
ness.   He is just a man, a human creature.   Adaptability, after all, is entirely a matter of environment.
The negroes have become skilled in the things their
hands have found to do.   Thus it happens—but it
only happens—that the negroes know how to plant,
cultivate, and harvest cotton better than any people
in the world, merely because they have the start of
the rest of the world by about a century.   That is
all.   They can learn other things in the same way,
and it is idle to suppose that the negro is limited
in his capacity in any particular direction.   The
Southern people must learn toleration, which will
be their salvation.   Whites as well as blacks in the
South need education in its broadest sense.   With
this they need the most advanced training in agriculture, to enable them to reach a thorough knowledge of the best use of the soil, the marvellous
soil, of the section where their lot has been cast.

" In the end, whatever may be the condition now,
the right of suffrage must be the sword and the
shield of all the people of a democracy.   In a
monarchy it is the duty of the nobles to guard, protect, and help the subject classes; but in a democracy
such as ours the ballot is absolutely the only pro-

174 The Negro and His Needs

tection of the citizen, and it is as necessary in the long run to the man whose skin is dark as to him whose skin is light. When the race question is properly settled, it can only be on the theory that the perpetuity of a nation depends upon the equality before the law of all its citizens. The coloured man may not need and may not get social equality, but he does need and should get equal treatment in the eye of the law, which is guaranteed to him by the Declaration of Independence and by the great and wise amendments to the Constitution of the United States."

## IV

## What Kind of Education?

I T is noticeable that all the negro leaders, in discussing the race problem, lay emphasis on the
need of education. No two of them, however,
seem to agree as to just what direction the educative
process should take. As we have seen, William H.
H. Hart advocates the common school, Booker T.
Washington the industrial institute, and Burghardt
DuBois desires not only both these but also institutions of higher learning, as a means of supply for
the teaching force of the lower schools. He claims
that there is no foundation for the constantly repeated assertion that the negro is deficient in the
reasoning faculty, hence cannot hope to receive the
benefits of higher education. According to his observation, the negro is capable of almost any intellectual achievement—a somewhat sweeping statement, which would hardly be true of any race of
white men, taken collectively. However, Dr. Du-
Bois defends his position thus:

" The negro is hampered at all times by the lack
of proper home training, by the traditions of a line
of uneducated ancestors, and by a timidity due to

his political and social status. As to his natural capabilities, however, the dull negro boy seems to be on a par with any other dull boy, and the bright negro is nearly identical with the bright white boy. I have watched the negro student study geometry, logic, and applied mathematics, going into matters in the arts and sciences where the active use of the reasoning faculty is indispensable, where nothing can be accomplished by mere memorizing.

" This same charge has been repeated many times and in many forms, and I am satisfied that it comes invariably from people who have not been actually engaged in teaching coloured children, but have worked only in executive positions, where they observe the mass of the coloured people but do not get at the individual at all. Few white people nowadays have the slightest chance to get at the negro at close range. Our more highly educated negroes are not brought into contact with the white people at all now; our coloured teachers, educated in the coloured colleges by coloured men and women, are teaching only coloured children, and the only white man they come in contact with officially is the superintendent of schools, with whom the relations are, of course, of the most formal character.

" There is a circle of coloured society in Atlanta all the members of which are well educated and well bred. They live by themselves, associate with each other, and do not mix with the whites in any way whatever. Among that class of people you will find the same mental development you find among people of the same class in Northern cities, making allowances only for peculiar social conditions and occasional lack of family training, which is perhaps the strongest feature in the culture of the white man."

What seems an argument in contradiction of the contention of Dr. DuBois that negro teachers are necessary for the lower schools among his people, is the fact that in Charleston at least they still find it necessary to employ white teachers to run the public schools for coloured pupils. An interesting feature in this case, throwing some light on the Southern view of social relations, is the refusal of the white teachers of coloured pupils in *public* schools to recognize or associate with the white teachers of coloured pupils in *private* schools, a sharp distinction being thus drawn between institutions to uplift the coloured people under government control, and those which are under the auspices of missionary societies and private individuals.

One at least of the group of educators who believe the negro incapable of higher education has not based his opinion on hasty judgment or general observation. Professor Otis Ashmore, for years superintendent of the city schools of Savannah, has been teaching in the schools of Georgia since 1876, and what he says grows out of personal touch with negro children.  At the time when I talked with him he had direct supervision of 6,500 white and 10,700 coloured children between six and eighteen years of age.  In all his work as an educator he has been among those who have, as he expressed it, " been sitting steady in the boat, doing the best they could to steer to some safe port."  He has studied especially the intellectual capacity of the negro as shown in his daily work in school, and the result is startling.

" I have found," he said, " that the negro is undoubtedly deficient in the reasoning faculty.  This is not an accident, but it is apparently constitutional. The negro children under my observation display considerable ability in matters which involve only perception and memory.  In fact, in harmony with the well-known law of compensation, the deficiency in the reasoning faculty frequently results in an added strength of memory.  Allowing for association and for defective home-training, the negro boy frequently, if not usually, shows the same capacity as the white boy in mere memorizing of lessons. It is at about the age of fourteen, as educators know, that the lessons in our schools begin to require the constant use of the reasoning faculty, and it is here that the negro boy begins to fall behind his white competitor.  He shows himself unquestionably deficient in logic. He is unable to argue from cause to effect, and when he cannot memorize he fails.

" This is not a temporary failing of the negro. It is not the result of social conditions, nor is it the result of slavery. It is clearly constitutional and probably racial, and sets a limit to the present achievements of the negro race. This bar may be removed by generations of training, but it does exist to-day. The generation with which we are dealing in the schools is at least the second since slavery, but the child is repeatedly like the father, comparatively easy to perceive, ready to memorize, but incapable of anything like real reasoning power.

" Some of our friends in the North have been pouring a good deal of money into institutions for the higher education of the negro. We have not discouraged this generosity and will not, but practically all that money is wasted, since for the reason I have stated, the deficiency in the reasoning faculty, the negro is unfitted for any real higher education. There are, of course, occasional exceptions to this rule, but in these exceptional cases the negro with anything more than a foundation of education finds it nearly impossible to get a position in which he can employ his knowledge. Even his own race will not hire him as a lawyer, a doctor, an architect, in any of the learned professions, or even in the arts. The negroes turn to the white man for all kinds of assistance, because they are sure that the white man is educated, and they suspect that their negro associate is not. The black men themselves are beginning dimly to realize the limit which nature has set upon their education.

" There is a distinct field for the employment of the negro. He imitates well, he learns how to do things with his own hands, and where it is a mere matter of observation, he makes a plodding but successful skilled mechanic. Here in Savannah we have negro carpenters, bricklayers, blacksmiths, plasterers, and other mechanical tradesmen. They do well wherever the trade is of such a character that it can be learned by observation; but wherever the trade requires the exercise of original reasoning faculties in the solving of mechanical problems, the negro is instantly at fault.

" The negro lacks prevision and provision. The farmer, of all people in the world, needs to look ahead. He must sow to-day in order to reap tomorrow; he must do things in one season which are to have results in another season. He is always anticipating the future. The negro simply finds it impossible to do this successfully. Hence he generally makes a failure as an independent farmer, although in other respects he has quite a genius for agriculture. When he has a white man to superintend his labours he gets along well, but when he is working for himself his farm soon runs down, and an investigation will inevitably show that the

failure is due to his constitutional inability to look
ahead. He will chop down a fruit tree in the winter regardless of the fact that it will deprive him
of the fruit in the summer; this is because it seems
necessary to him to sacrifice the fruit tree as during
the warm weather he forgot to cut wood for the
winter. This lack of the reasoning faculty runs
through all the negroes, and hence it is I have
become convinced that the salvation of the race,
if there is a salvation, depends upon their receiving
first of all a common-school education, supplemented with manual training in all the mechanical
arts which can be learned by observation and imitation, and without the use of the reasoning faculty.

"White blood tells in the negro every time. It
is frequently the case that an apparently black man
shows a certain remarkable strength of character,
and upon inquiry it is generally found that a comparatively remote ancestor was white. The union
with the white man does promote intellectual activity as a matter of course; though often this intellectual activity is grossly misdirected, because
the combination is not natural, and the white man's
mind is mixed up with the negro's lack of it. The
hybrid race is apparently in most cases physically
inferior to both the white and the black races. The
combination, therefore, of an increased mental activity with a weak physical condition is far from
desirable. The black people, however, long to be

white, and there is a persistent tendency among the black men to affiliate themselves with the yellow girls; the lighter the bride, the more glory there is in the attachment.

" No man can predict the future of the black race. Many Southern people are entirely hopeless as to the good effect of any education whatever upon the blacks. Naturally, as an educator, I take the ground that knowledge is better than ignorance under all conditions. We should make an effort first of all to remove the actual illiteracy of the negro. The higher education of the few is entirely useless in the face of the gross ignorance of the masses. The educated negro must depend for his livelihood upon his own race; but he cannot secure support from them until they are comparatively self-sustaining, and they cannot be that until they have the groundwork of an education. As to the education of the masses, they need most of all a mere foundation in reading, writing, spelling, and ordinary mathematics, the bare common-school branches. This should be immediately supplemented by careful instruction in the use of the hands, a general industrial education, and training in ordinary scientific agriculture. All this should be done by practical lessons, where the imitative faculty of the negro can be made available, and almost nothing should be left to his reason.

" The negro seems to make an admirable mechanic. He has the use of his hands to an extraordinary degree, is comparatively docile, and if he has a good teacher makes a good pupil, because he is a good imitator. Here in Savannah they have gone into almost all the ordinary trades. They have no success at all in the arts, because they have no creative faculty whatever. A negro painter will lay on a colour successfully, but he cannot suggest shades nor create colour combinations. Many of the negro artisans here join trade unions of their own, but their allegiance does not sit heavily upon them. The negro is no general, he cannot plan a campaign, and he cannot combine successfully. This makes him a failure as a trade unionist, but it does not affect his individual workmanship, which is generally good.

" Here in Savannah the negro population pays less than two per cent of the entire taxation. We have in this State a poll tax which goes to the support of the schools, and as only a fraction of the negro population pay this tax, while they pay practically nothing in real estate and personal taxes, which also go to support the public schools, it is evident that the burden of lifting the negro race out of its condition of profound ignorance has to be borne by the white people of the South. They are doing the best they can, but it must be remembered that it is their duty to educate the white children, quite as much as the black children.

" Northern people who complain of the continued illiteracy of the negro shut their eyes to the fact that the money the Northern people contribute for the education of the negro goes to schools and colleges, while the Southern white people, many of whom are still staggering under the blighting effect of the Civil War, are compelled not only to endure the presence of the negroes, but to educate them as well in the common-school branches, which is all that the great mass of the negro population has any time for. It is a fact which it is well to stop and ponder upon, that one coloured institution, the University of Atlanta, has a larger endowment to-day, and more funds at its disposal, than all the higher institutions for the education of all the white people in the entire State of Georgia."

A broader view of the possibilities of negro education is taken by Dr. H. B. Frissell, well known as the head of the Hampton Normal and Agricultural Institute founded by General Armstrong. There are probably few men in the country so well qualified to speak intelligently as to the mental capacity of the negro. And that subject is worth enlightened attention, for it is evident that if the negro is capable of being mentally trained to any degree, his moral and physical condition will in a few generations be so improved that he will no longer be a menace to the community.

As we have seen, Southern men, educators,

editors, statesmen, and business men alike, unite to
say that the negro whom they know so well at close
range has a deficient mental organism and is con-
stitutionally unable to approximate the white man's
culture, while Booker Washington and Burghardt
DuBois are either freaks or products of the white
strain.    It is noteworthy, then, when a man like
Dr. Frissell, a trained educator, a graduate of Yale,
and the principal of the institution which graduated
Booker Washington and which is still sending out
teachers to Tuskegee and almost every other coloured school, declares that this expression of opinion of the Southern men is not founded upon facts.
The Hampton school is manned almost exclusively
by white teachers, and the day of enthusiastic missionary influence has gone by, so that the negro is
being studied there from a purely professional educational standpoint.    The officers and teachers of
the Hampton school, including many from the
South, unite in the declaration that while the percentage of ignorance among the negroes in America
is startling, the individuals that can be reached by
patient instruction respond with even more readi-
ness than densely ignorant white people.    Their investigations are full of hope for negroes and whites
alike, because they show that with intelligent and
persistent effort the black people can be raised to a
condition at least approximate to that of their white
neighbours.

Dr. Frissell's philosophical analysis of the race question is worthy of thoughtful study both North and South. In contact with the negro day after day and year after year, he has been able to study his living problem and his character without the prejudice of the Southern white and without the long distance ignorance of the Northern white.

"There is no dead line in negro education," was Dr. Frissell's first proposition. "That is, there is no limit to the possible culture of the negro race as a whole. There is a jumping-off place in education for all races, white or black, brown or yellow. That is to say, there is a place at which a great mass of the race stops, and only the individual goes beyond it. The negro is undeniably inferior to the Anglo-Saxon; there can be no question as to that; but the inferiority is a matter of training, of heredity, of association, and of opportunity. When we reach the ordinary jumping-off place, there is a vastly greater number of white individuals than of black ones that will leap over the barrier, but no set boundary can be placed to the individual's capacity for culture, in either race.

"My observations during years of close contact with the negro do not lead me to believe at all that there is any constitutional limitation to the mental capacity of his race. On the contrary, there is a certain amount of receptivity which is quite marked in the negro. Once you get him interested he learns readily, and within certain bounds progresses about as well as the average white boy with the same lack of home training.  Nor is there any apparent difference between the full-blooded negro and the mulatto, except so far as the lighter coloured negro has associated more with the whites, owing to his having been chosen for indoor employment.  We have for years endeavoured to trace the work of the full-blooded negro as compared with the mixed blood.  I cannot see that we have established any difference between them.  On the contrary, our valedictorians run all the way from the blackest negro to the lightest mulatto who would pass for white anywhere in the Northern States."

The acute observations of Dr. Frissell on slavery and the results of emancipation would go a long way toward explaining some of the problems which have troubled the friends of the negro and gratified his enemies.  " Slavery," he said, " had its good features and uses as well as its bad ones.  While it kept negroes from being educated, it also kept them from being criminal.  The institution of slavery put all the negroes on a dead level.  The black men with criminal and vicious instincts were forced like all the rest to be industrious.  They had no opportunity to commit crime, and if they broke over the bounds were punished so relentlessly that they were speedily cowed into subjection.  In this way, slavery as a matter of course prevented crime to a great extent. When emancipation came, the naturally depraved and criminal class of negroes was let loose and deprived of this restraining influence of the slavery system. Such men began, naturally, to confound license with liberty, and they have distinctly degenerated since slavery days.

" It is this degenerate, naturally criminal class among the negroes which is giving us all the trouble to-day. They are not any more numerous proportionately than the same class of criminals in any other race. They are the single ' submerged tenth ' among the negroes, and are practically identical in their criminal instincts and their criminal following with the same class that we find in the white slums of New York and Chicago. Their number is not growing, but, on the contrary, is being reduced by the advance of education in the South.

" On the other hand, we are entirely familiar with the distinctly bad effect of slavery, in its involving the denial of education to the negro. In fact, slavery could not exist with an educated, cultured class of slaves. So a large proportion of the negroes, capable of a fair measure of culture, were reduced to the same level, by slavery, with the incompetent and criminal class. Since emancipation, this portion of the coloured race, so far as it could be reached by the purely voluntary educational methods that the country has been satisfied to adopt, has made enormous strides. Washington, DuBois, and many other negroes whose names have become familiar to white men are not freaks, but are merely examples of what education has done and will do for that great class of negroes whose natural mental activity was reduced by slavery to the natural dead level. Such negroes have advanced as no other race in the history of the world ever did advance in the same length of time. They have had the advantage of association with cultured white men, which no other barbaric race ever had. The negro has shown himself susceptible of education, and it is impossible for us to deny the fact. Therefore the negroes themselves should not lose hope, even if for the present they do not secure all the rights they consider themselves entitled to.

" Furthermore, we must not lose sight of the fact that there was a great middle class of negroes, midway between the progressive and criminal elements, which was neither helped nor hindered by emancipation. This great intermediate stratum is to-day about where it was a generation ago—at the dead level to which slavery compressed the whole race. It is this element, which is neither criminal nor intellectual, which is merely inert, that we have to train into good citizenship by education. For the great mass of coloured people, work with their hands must continue to be the only thing they can do successfully. It is in harmony with this idea that we have laid such stress here in Hampton upon

agriculture. Our academic course is entirely sub-
sidiary. It merely seeks to teach the pupil how to
become a better farmer. In our industrial department we have been laying more and more stress
upon those trades which can be practised more
easily in connection with agriculture. Blacksmiths,
wheelwrights, ordinary carpenters, and similar simple mechanics can find ready occupation in farming
districts.

" We have deemed it best to maintain a white
faculty in this school for coloured children for a
variety of reasons. The most important, perhaps, is
that the negro for a long time to come must expect
to reap the benefit of the culture and experience of
the white man. If we were to turn the negroes
loose to educate themselves exclusively there would
be but little progress. It seems to be necessary, in
fact, to keep a constant stream of white culture
pouring in, if we are to secure the best results. We
find that association with cultivated white teachers
is an excellent thing for the young negro boys and
girls. They learn a great deal by mere imitation,
and they readily appreciate the fact that the culture
of the white man, which has made him what he is,
is being freely put at their disposal."

This question of the influence of white teachers
upon coloured students can perhaps be best understood from the fact that Booker Washington is a
graduate of Hampton, and that the Hampton school

sends coloured teachers annually to Tuskegee and other negro institutions, which are exclusively manned by coloured men and women. In truth, it was General Armstrong at Hampton who, on request of the people of Alabama, selected Booker Washington to organize the school which has made such a vast success so much farther South, under the exclusive control of negro teachers.

Dr. Frissell went on to speak of the delicate social relations between the white teachers and the negro scholars.

" I wish our friends in the South could learn the lesson we have learned here, which is that when the negro is really cultivated and taught self-respect he prefers to keep to himself, to associate with other cultivated negroes, and does not bother the white people at all. It is not true that the moment you attempt to cultivate the negro, you instil into him notions of social equality. Quite the contrary is true. When we succeed in teaching the coloured men and women self-respect, from that moment they begin to realize that there is something in their own race to be proud of. They seek the society of coloured people with similar ideals, and they never make the slightest attempt to cultivate social relations with white people of the vicinity."

# V

## The Great Need

TAKING the consensus of opinion among those who are striving for the uplift of the negro, we may arrive at the belief that the most practicable method of solving the race problem is the method of education, of a kind adapted to the peculiar temperament and needs of the black race. Not only justice and humanity call for it, but expediency as well. For apparently the only way to prevent the evil effects of the negro domination which the South dreads is to educate, educate, educate. The Southerner will scoff at this statement. He takes the position that the negro is so nearly savage he cannot be bettered; he honestly believes that the slightest tinge of education not only destroys the usefulness of the negro as a labourer, but injures him morally and makes him a menace to the community. For the most part the South looks on the negro merely as a familiar domestic animal, whose slothful ignorance has for generations been a matter of indifference. But the intelligent Southerners who really have the interests of the negro at heart are sincere in their belief that the more the black man is educated the worse he is off. Such a theory is an extraordinary absurdity; it is even more dangerous than the Northern notion that the betterment of the negro is to be found in the ballot box. For in all this the South is manifestly not alive to the situation; it is deficient in its own civilization; it is a half century behind the great prosperous States of the North in its educational methods.

The little red schoolhouse, unfortunately, is not a familiar sight in the country districts in the Southern States. Every one knows that the negroes are hopelessly ignorant at the present time; not every one is aware of the fact that the means of education for white children as well, in the purely agricultural districts of the South, are such as would create a scandal in Massachusetts, or in New York, or in Iowa. Throughout the length and breadth of the South there is a crying need of awakened and enlightened public opinion on the subject of education. Since the white people have been so backward in educating their own children, it is not surprising that they consider the education of the negro worse than superfluous.

In view of the things to which the Southern people have had to submit, from the changed conditions growing out of the war, they undoubtedly treat the negro with great fairness. They are much more lenient toward his petty faults than is the North;

but on the other hand, they seem to betray a selfish interest in keeping him as far as possible below the white race. It is a rare thing to find a Southern man or woman who is earnestly engaged in bettering the mental condition of the coloured people. They will look after the negro's housing conditions, they will try to teach him to be economical, they will give him better clothes, they will provide him with food, in a queer kind of way they will even supervise his morals; but they will not educate him. And though the best fruits of Hampton and Tuskegee, of Howard and Atlanta Universities, have given the lie to the mediæval theory that education can injure any class, and have proved that the black man can be educated, it yet seems impossible to teach the Southerner that the kind of education which will convert an ignorant and frequently criminal immigrant from southeast Europe into a good citizen will in the course of time do the same thing for the negro.

If the negro is lazy, idle, childish, filthy, imprudent, grossly immoral, it is largely because of his ignorance of the ways of the industrious, intelligent, moral world. That ignorance can only be remedied by the blessing of a common school education. It seems probable that an investigation of cases of assault by negroes will show in nine cases out of ten that the negro guilty of the terrible crime is densely ignorant. So far as I know, there has been no authenticated case where a really educated negro, who has been thrown into close contact with educated white people, has been guilty of such a deed.

There is not a single Southern State where half the negroes can read and write. The percentage of illiteracy varies; it is lowest in Florida and Texas, highest in Louisiana and Alabama, particularly in the sugar and cotton country. But the census figures by no means represent the symmetrical ignorance of the Southern negro. Tens of thousands of the number who claim to be able to read and write can do nothing more than spell out their names, or work over odd verses in the Bible. There are not ten per cent of the agricultural negroes in the South who possess even the rudiments of a grammar school education. Whenever the negro can get to the city he is apt to find a school, but the black people of the rural districts in the South are almost wholly unprovided with means for educating their children.

When I have asked coloured people why they wanted to get away from the country, where they were well taken care of, to the city, where they live in hovels, the invariable answer has been that they hoped to educate their children, and could not do so in the country. This desire for education, which in many instances is merely an ignorant belief that education brings freedom from work, is widespread among the coloured people, and whatever may be its cause, the sentiment must be placed to the credit of the race.

These black people in their horrible ignorance, are a menace to the prosperity and the peace of the Southern States. They are, at the same time, a disgrace to the nation, because these black people are citizens of the United States quite as much as they are citizens of South Carolina or Florida. It is safe to say they will not be educated for long generations to come, unless the national government takes a hand in the operation.

The South was never any too rich, as regards the mass of its white people; its wealth was always concentrated among the wealthy planter class. Even of that wealth it was despoiled by the war. Its fields were desolated, its plantations ruined, its capital dissipated, and its young men made old before their time, through the hardships of soldiery. To-day the South is prosperous, but it has no reserve capital of its own. In fact, it is just beginning to save. Its public funds are small; its tax levies are necessarily meagre; its needs are great. It will take still a generation or two to make up the vast monetary losses of the Civil War. In the face of all this, it finds itself with a growing negro population of many millions. To ask the South, unaided, to educate these negroes would be a cruel injustice; and indeed, it is impossible to believe that the few rich people in the South would tax themselves to attempt to educate millions upon millions of the blacks who were once their slaves. Any effort on the part of the government to saddle the education of the black mass upon the little white minority would mean surely bankruptcy, possibly rebellion. And the negroes obviously cannot educate themselves; they are hopelessly poor and pitifully ignorant. It is plain that there is need for a movement on the part of the whole nation toward the uplift and education of the negro race.

The national government should do the educating. Why would it not be feasible to establish a national educational fund, by the authority of the federal government, taxing the people of the United States as a whole, and apportioning the fund among the States on the basis of illiteracy? The fund need not be limited to white illiterates nor to negro illiterates, but could be made general in its scope, and could be apportioned on the basis of ignorance among men or women, or both, of voting age.

If we can stamp out yellow fever or smallpox by authority of the national government, why can we not stamp out illiteracy by the same authority? Why not inoculate the whole negro race with the bacillus of education? Put a country schoolhouse within easy walking distance of every group of negro cabins; compel every little darkey between the ages of six and sixteen to go to school a prescribed number of weeks in every year. The result would be in a single generation of time the creation of a new American negro race.

Though most Southern men oppose the idea of the negro's education as they opposed the idea of his freedom, they have all welcomed this suggestion. They think that if there must be education at all, it is the place of the national government, in all fairness, to attend to the matter. It is hardly necessary to argue the justice of such a plan. It was New England people who brought the first slaves to this country; it was Northern bayonets which were responsible for the shocking excesses of the reconstruction period in the South immediately after the war. If the black man in the South is ignorant, degraded, immoral, improvident, and dense, it is largely the fault of the North, which struck the shackles from his feet, and then left him to shift for himself, a hopeless foundling in an unfriendly world. Those were blind and blundering statesmen, who, having freed the negro, made not the slightest provision for his mental and moral uplifting. As a matter of pure theory, they conferred upon him the useless privilege of the ballot and then left him alone. From that day to this there has been no systematic effort to cultivate the mental apparatus of the Afro-American.

The great, rich, progressive, educated North should at last wake up to the real necessities of the

negro question. The black man did not come to
America of himself. He is not an immigrant. He
was brought here by force; and it is only fair that
he should be given at least an equal chance in the
community. It is quite feasible and it is entirely
legal for the nation to attack the terrible illiteracy
of the South, and it should do so without regard
either for the obsolete opposition of the Southern
whites or for the ignorant indifference of the Southern blacks.

To a certain extent the Southern people are quite
right in their opposition to the education of the
negro. The negro leaders who want universities
instead of schoolhouses, treatises on logic and tables
of logarithms instead of spelling books and arith-
metics, are but another illustration of the familiar
truth that " a little knowledge is a dangerous thing."
The higher education of the negro at the present
time seems like an attempt to put on the roof before
work is begun on the foundation. Many Northern
philanthropists have made a great mistake in spend-
ing so much money on colleges and universities for
the coloured people. To a large extent these institutions are absurd. Judging from my present im-
perfect study of the race question in this country,
the best plan would be to abolish all but one or
two of the so-called negro colleges, or at least to
consolidate them into one or two institutions, sufficient to afford an outlet for such brilliant, intelli-

gent abnormalities as Professor DuBois in Atlanta, and a few other negroes who begin to approach him in general culture.

What the negroes need in the way of literary schools could be supplied by a few institutions of the ordinary normal school type, a kind of school familiar throughout the best educated States in the North. A high school training is quite sufficient for ordinary grammar school teachers, with a year or two of a normal course as an addition. These normal and high schools are absolutely all that will be needed by the negroes for two or three generations to come, with one or two colleges to provide for the aspirations of the few who desire to pursue their studies further.

For the great mass of the negroes the need to-day is for a genuine system of primary schools. We should teach the agricultural labourer and the toiler in the city how to read and how to write, how to add two and two and to count to one thousand. We should teach him how to make change and how to read an ordinary contract. We should teach him how to write a plain, readable letter, how to give a receipt, and how to make out a bill. Then we should let him alone.

Side by side with this primary school and grammar school education there should be manual training for the negro, of the sort being done by Booker Washington and by the splendid school at Hampton, where that great negro himself was educated. Combine this industrial education with the grammar school training indicated, and there will be open to the negro race that opportunity for self-respect and capable service in the world which is now denied it.

Great care must be taken to avoid the super-education of the negro. And this word of warning is especially directed to many estimable philanthropists, who are willing to attach their names to colleges, but are slow to devote their money to the multiplication of humble little country schools. The field hand does not need to know Latin, and he may well be ignorant of the chemistry of the soil; but he does need to know how to use his hands, how to detect fraud in a labour contract, how to scrutinize his account at a plantation store, and above all, how to write his name, so that he shall not be made the victim of his own lack of knowledge. Most of the ills of the negro in the South to-day are brought about by his own consuming ignorance; and it is to be feared that some of the Southern opposition to his education is born of a selfish desire to utilize his ignorance for his continued enslavement.

Stop the coloured university just where it is. Don't starve it; but don't build any more, and don't increase the endowment of the existing ones until illiteracy has been practically stamped out. Put a little red schoolhouse within sight of every planta-

202 The Negro and His Needs

tion, and give the children time to go to school. Prohibit employment of boys and girls on the plantations except during the summer months, and require the little darkies to put in a certain number of weeks in school. Multiply institutions like the Tuskegee and Hampton industrial schools, and endow them with funds by the national government. Put one such school in every black county in the Southern States. Teach reading, writing, arithmetic, geography, and little else from books. Teach blacksmithing and the use of the hammer; teach reasonable, sensible agricultural methods; and then turn the negro boy and girl loose, to teach their younger brothers and sisters the same thing.

The older generations of the black people in the South cannot be reached to-day, I believe, by any possible system of education; but the little children, boys and girls, are actually hungry for schooling. They will respond to the effort instantly, and in fifty years the illiteracy of the black people of the South, which is to-day a disgrace to the civilization of America, could readily be wiped out.

# DEDUCTIONS

# DEDUCTIONS

IN summing up the results of this study of the negro question, there are a few conclusions to be drawn. Throughout the investigation it has become more and more evident that what was stated in the beginning is true—the South is too near the negro and the North too far away from him for the position of either to be the true one. There is, however, a safe middle ground somewhere, on which the North and South will ultimately unite in the decision of what is best for the negro. North and South are both to blame for the present disagreeable situation, and each must modify its point of view to reach an accurate and enduring settlement. The negro is a human being, capable of rapid improvement, and destined in the end to participation in the actual management of the republic. The South must awake to this, and stop thinking of the negro as a despised bondsman or as a mere domestic animal. The North must abandon its hysterical attitude; it must beware of making matters worse. It must admit that the negro as a race is not the equal of the white man, and that until he approximates the Caucasian in general racial intelligence, he cannot safely be entrusted with full political power.

Meanwhile, in seeking for the desired middle ground, the most important thing to be observed, in my belief, is the necessity for extreme caution in disturbing present conditions. The negro in the South is out of politics now; let him stay out a bit longer. He is not helped by appointment to important political office. On the contrary, it is only when he is out of politics that he can hope to secure the support of his white neighbours, without which his uplifting must be impossible. The ballot does not help the negro to secure work, nor to educate his children. He is much too ignorant to apply the remedy of the suffrage to disperse the evil of his present condition. What the negro in the South most needs to-day is not the ballot but the spelling-book.

The manifest future of the negro race in America lies along the line of mental and industrial culture. Booker T. Washington is right, and Burghardt DuBois and T. Thomas Fortune are dangerously wrong. The negro editors of the North, who write inflammatory editorials which are circulated among the ignorant plantation hands, are not the real friends of the black race. Booker T. Washington has had to win his victories devoid of the sympathy and support of the leaders of his own race. Yet, in some strange way, this great negro, a century ahead of his own people in intellectual grasp of a complex situation, sees clearly that the black man must be equipped to fight the real battles of the world, that he must learn economy and frugality, that he must acquire property, and that he must make for himself a place in the community from which he cannot be dislodged.

The South needs more and better labour. The industrial and commercial development of that section cannot proceed without a much more abundant labour supply, which can be secured only through encouragement of white immigration from Europe. Iron and coal will not come out of the ground of themselves, and the negro population of the South is to-day wholly insufficient even to till the fields. But foreign white labour will not go to the South until conditions there as to the treatment of labouring men are greatly bettered. That can be done only by bettering the condition of the negro himself, so that foreign white men will be content to work by his side.

Lynchings, I firmly believe, are ephemeral episodes, so far as the great race question is concerned. An accurate record of all such outbreaks will show beyond peradventure that the great majority were not provoked by the crime of assault, nor even by insults to white women. On the contrary, in four out of five cases noted in the newspapers it will be discovered that negroes were lynched for robberies, arson, attacks upon white men, and even for mere threats. There are, unfortunately, too many cases of assault upon white women and children by negro men, but the number is extremely small as compared with the number of lynchings. It is also suspicious that whenever a lynching party starts out on a search for a criminal, it "generally gets some nigger," as one of my informants put it. That is to say, no man can tell how many times the wrong negro is lynched.

White men are not lynched in the South. What is more, a white man who kills a white man in the South is not ordinarily punished by process of law. This is a sweeping statement, but the files of Southern newspapers will prove it true. The pistol-carrying habit in the South is a disgrace to that community. It began among the whites, and has now been generally adopted by the negroes themselves. The South ought to put a stop to it at once. It should punish the carrying of concealed weapons with a term in the penitentiary, and it should try and hang murderers according to the law and the evidence, whether they be white or black. If that be done, and if the lynchings are limited to the proved cases of outrageous assault upon women, the necessity for these illegal murders will soon disappear, as the process of education tends to eliminate

the one great crime which has been made the justification for lynchings. When the South improves
its general administration of criminal law, and ap-
plies it equally to white and black, lynchings themselves will cease as merely ephemeral manifesta-
tions of a disjointed race episode.

A few brief suggestions, serving to sum up the
policy of the nation toward the negro and his needs
may not be out of place in conclusion.

Deprive the negro of his commanding position
as the sole labour supply of the South. Dignify the
condition of labour by elevating the condition of
the negro, and thus encourage the immigration of
white labour, to relieve the congestion, to develop
Southern industries, and to civilize the negro by
contact.

Educate the negro at the expense of the whole
nation. Put a little black schoolhouse within sound
of every plantation bell.

Stop public negro education with the grammar
school, and let all higher education be at private
expense.

Plant industrial schools of the Tuskegee and
Hampton type in every black county of the
South.

Keep the negro out of politics in the South until
the average of the race is at least equal to that of
the European immigrant of to-day. Do this by any
means satisfactory to the rough and ready Anglo-

Saxon mind, and patch up the constitution afterwards.

Lynch no negro for anything except crimes against women, and then be sure you have the right negro.

Hang a few white men for murder now and then, just as an example to their poor black neighbours.

Sew up every pistol pocket south of Mason and Dixon's line.

Chain up all anarchistic negro editors north of that line, and put in comfortable asylums Southern statesmen who oppose the education of the negro.

Teach the negro as a man, and not as a baby, punish him when he does wrong, reward him for right living, but above all teach him morality and justice by the example of the white man.

Stop whining about the immorality of the negro until there are to be seen no more mulatto children with white fathers.

Remember always that the negro did not come to America of his own accord, that he has but recently escaped from the degradation of slavery, and that his vices and his follies, harassing though they be, certainly can be removed by wise educational methods, adapted to his condition, and persisted in for years and for generations.

Do these things to-day, and to-morrow the race question will disappear.

The negro himself, meanwhile, must be patient. As a race he is not yet able to decide what is best for him. He is a babe in arms, so far as the civilized world is concerned, and if he does not obey, it is likely the big world will compel him to do so by the exercise of unpleasant force. In a word, he is not likely to have much voice in the settlement of the race question for some time to come. The tail seldom does much toward guiding the footsteps of the dog. The Indian was exterminated because he resisted the irresistible. Though the negro is as ignorant as ever the Indian was, he is by nature tractable, so that he is destined to a slow process of improvement rather than a rapid one of annihilation.

In conclusion, the country must not forget the complications of the race question. There are issues at stake involving politics, education, labour, immigration, industrial and agricultural necessities, all of which must be settled long before we reach the great issue of possible social equality, which, after all, for the present century, is only the fabric of a dream.

Finally, let me reiterate the declaration that the only permanent settlement of the race question in America must come through the education of the negro; that this must proceed from the ground up through the district school, and not through the university; and that the people of New York, and of

Illinois, and of Oregon are quite as responsible for negro illiteracy as the people of Georgia and Arkansas.

The uplifting of the negro must be done by the nation.

THE END